REPORTING UNDER FIRE

16 Daring Women War Correspondents
and Photojournalists

KERRIE LOGAN HOLLIHAN

CHICAGO
REVIEW
PRESS

Copyright © 2014 by Kerrie L. Hollihan
All rights reserved
First edition
Published by Chicago Review Press, Incorporated
814 North Franklin Street
Chicago, Illinois 60610

ISBN 978-1-61374-710-0

Cover and interior design: Sarah Olson

Library of Congress Cataloging-in-Publication Data

Hollihan, Kerrie Logan.
  Reporting under fire : 16 daring women war correspondents and
photojournalists / Kerrie Logan Hollihan. — First edition.
    pages cm. — (Women of action)
  Summary: "'The tremendous struggles women have faced as war
correspondents and photojournalists A profile of 16 courageous women,
Reporting Under Fire tells the story of journalists who risked their lives to bring
back scoops from the front lines. Each woman—including Sigrid Schultz, who
broadcast news via radio from Berlin on the eve of the Second World War;
Margaret Bourke-White, who rode with General George Patton's Third Army
and brought back the first horrific photos of the Buchenwald concentration
camp; and Marguerite Higgins, who typed stories while riding in the front seat
of an American jeep that was fleeing the North Korean Army—experiences
her own journey, both personally and professionally, and each draws her own
conclusions. Yet without exception, these war correspondents share a singular
ambition: to answer an inner call driving them to witness war firsthand, and to
share what they learn via words or images"—Provided by publisher.
  Includes bibliographical references and index.
  ISBN 978-1-61374-710-0 (hardback)
  1. Women journalists—United States—Biography—Juvenile literature. 2. War
photographers—United States—Biography—Juvenile literature 3. Women
photographers—United States—Biography—Juvenile literature I. Title.

PN4872.H65 2014
070.4333092'52--dc23
[B]
                                        2013048102

Contents

A Note to Readers

When my daughter was a junior at Saint Ursula Academy in Cincinnati, someone wrote a lovely quote on a poster during pep week. It was from Judy Garland, a film star and singer who first captured Americans' hearts as Dorothy in *The Wizard of Oz* back in 1939. It said: "Always be a first-rate version of yourself instead of a second-rate version of somebody else."

I think that's excellent advice, and Garland's words came to me as I was putting the finishing touches on this book. In looking over the profiles I'd researched and written over nearly a year, I was struck by how each of these women is (or was) so much her authentic self. Of course, times have changed, as they always do, and the "girl reporter" like Peggy Hull, who was ordered to write a womanly slant on war stories, has been replaced by the likes of Martha Raddatz, who has jumped from a helicopter when her job demanded it.

As individuals, these women were as different as could be. Some of them were better at digging out information than at writing it; others were or are gifted writers. Some were fiercely left-wing, some kept to the middle, and others wore their conservatism proudly. Some treasured their privacy, while others were quite flamboyant. Beyond one or two, you've probably never read their names, though several were celebrities in their day. Their stories are worth telling—and remembering—though most of these women have come and gone since the first were born in the 1880s.

There is so much truth in these women's stories, and it's not just the truth they told in the articles they wrote and the photographs they took. To read their letters, their books and memoirs, and their reporting is to share in their personal journeys of truth and self-discovery. In the process of putting their stories on paper, I discovered that, like a first love, there was a "first war" for each, a time for truth-telling both inside and out. For the most part, I've focused on that piece of their lives.

INTRODUCTION

The Race
to Be First

In the news business there's long been a race to be first, the classic contest among rival media to "scoop" the competition. In the 1800s and first half of the 1900s, when the scooper happened to be a woman, that made news, too. In 1887, a brash young reporter named Elizabeth Cochrane managed to get herself committed to an insane asylum on New York's Blackwell's Island, a living hell for its mentally ill inmates. Ten days later she emerged and wrote about her experiences under the pen name "Nellie Bly" for the *New York World*. She had scooped every other New York paper with her outrageous exposé, and the *World* loudly paraded her as its "stunt girl." Nellie Bly became America's first big name among investigative journalists who wore dresses to work.

Historians of American journalism have ferreted out more women "firsts." Among them were the first woman to publish a newspaper (Elizabeth Timothy of the *South Carolina Gazette*, 1759); the first to publish the full, official Declaration of Independence (Mary Katherine Goddard of the *Maryland Journal*, 1777); the first woman to edit a national magazine (Sarah Josepha Hale of *Godey's Ladies Book*, 1836); and the first woman editor at a daily newspaper (Cornelia Walter of the *Boston Transcript*, 1842). The outspoken Anne Newport Royall, a rabble-rouser and writer during the 1820s and '30s, probably holds the claim as the nation's first official woman reporter.

Historians also have looked back to decide who could be called America's first woman war correspondent. She was probably Margaret Fuller, a rare bird among women in the years before the American Civil War. Fuller was a full-fledged intellectual and free thinker. Her remarkable writing—like a man's, in fact—appalled many men who dominated America's literary circles. But she had her male admirers too, and one, a newspaper editor named Horace Greeley, hired her to send dispatches—letters—from Europe as she witnessed the Italian revolution

in 1847. In the process, Fuller found love and had a child with an Italian count. All three perished when their ship sank just offshore as they returned to the United States.

Margaret Fuller, a philosopher and woman of letters, was probably America's first woman war correspondent. *Library of Congress LC-USZ62-47039*

World traveler Elizabeth Cochrane, "Nellie Bly," was heralded as a stunt reporter for the *New York World*.
Library of Congress
LC-USZ62-59924

There were others. During the Civil War, a Southern woman known to the world only as "Joan" left her home to be near her son, a Confederate soldier in Virginia. To support herself, Joan wrote for the *Charleston Courier*, her pen name a protection because well-bred ladies weren't supposed to dirty themselves with work. In the North, Jane Swisshelm owned her own newspaper in Minnesota before the Civil War and was said to have reported on events as she nursed Union soldiers near Washington, DC.

Not exactly a war correspondent but a globetrotter nonetheless, Nellie Bly famously circled the world in seventy-two days in 1889, topping the fictitious record set by Phileas Fogg in Jules Verne's *Around the World in Eighty Days*. And *Leslie's Illustrated Weekly* dispatched Anna Benjamin to Cuba during the Spanish-American War in 1898, where she became the nation's first female photojournalist.

For the better part of the 1800s, Victorian ideals confined middle- and upper-class American women to home, a sphere of domesticity where women ran their households and raised their children. However, late in the century, Victorian rules loosened, and some women stepped into the workplace in their high-button shoes. They filled traditional roles as teachers and nurses and also took jobs in factories or as clerks in offices and department stores. Women were a common sight at newspapers, although they were confined to working on the ever more popular "women's pages." The gritty job of reporting on crime, corruption, and general evil on the streets wasn't thought to be ladylike. "Girl reporters," as newspapermen called them, weren't welcome to work at the city desk, the heart and soul of a daily newspaper.

Given that women rarely wrote hard news at home in the United States, it was even more of a reach for a young girl to dream of reporting from overseas. But as the 19th century rolled into the 20th, and as more and more girls got an education, a few began to think beyond the boundaries set for women just 20 years earlier. After all, there were fashion stories to be written from Paris and society news from London, and so a few young women reporters found their way to Europe. And when male reporters flocked overseas in 1917 to cover the American Expeditionary Force in the Great War, a handful of young women followed them to the front lines. All kinds of obstacles stood in their way, namely editors at home and army officials both at home and overseas. It was unthinkable that someone wearing a skirt had any business in a battle zone.

1

World War I
1914–1918

In the early hours of June 29, 1914, transatlantic cable traffic from Europe buzzed with reports from the tiny nation of Serbia, far away in the Balkans. Editors on the foreign desks of big American newspapers rolled up their sleeves and got to work to rush the news onto their front pages: the Austrian archduke Franz Ferdinand and his wife, the duchess Sophie, had been assassinated during a state visit to Sarajevo, Serbia's capital.

On July 28, exactly one month after the assassination, Austria-Hungary declared war on Serbia. That single declaration triggered all-out war across Europe as a complex set of treaties lunged into motion. Nine days later, most of Europe was at war—Germany and Austria-Hungary (the Central powers) battling France, Great Britain, Italy, and Russia (the Allied powers). Both sides expected the fighting to be short and glorious, but on

August 22, when 27,000 French soldiers died on a single day in the opening battles, reality began to hit home.

Under President Woodrow Wilson's isolationist policies, the United States tried to stay out of Europe's Great War, but in April 1917, Americans were finally sucked into the bloody conflict. Untried and idealistic, American youths left cities and farms to fight "the war to end all wars." The American Expeditionary Force, commanded by General John "Black Jack" Pershing, arrived in France that summer. Pershing came fresh from his previous command a year earlier when he had led American soldiers into Mexico to capture the bandit Pancho Villa.

American reporters secured credentials from the US government and followed troops into France. All were men. *A war was no place for a woman*, went the thinking of the time. After all, few women had broken through the invisible wall that blockaded "girl reporters" from the tobacco-spitting environs of the city desk. Although it was the era of the "New Woman" in the United States and American women had made some progress in filling professional jobs since 1900, in 1917 they still did not even have the right to vote.

Only a handful of women made their way into war zones as battles raged in France. With the backing of the *Saturday Evening Post*, Mary Roberts Rinehart, a popular mystery writer, went to the front early in the war and was appalled at the dreadful medical care available for wounded soldiers. Another, a photographer named Helen Johns Kirtland, went to France on her honeymoon, got to the trenches, and took memorable photographs. Peggy Hull, who had mistakenly upstaged Pershing in Texas, sidestepped the ban on women reporters and went to France as well.

Henrietta Goodnough, aka Peggy Hull

REPORTING FROM EL PASO, PARIS, AND VLADIVOSTOK

It was July 4, 1917. . . . I was in Paris [sitting in a sidewalk café with two Frenchwomen. Suddenly] . . . a low murmur reached our ears . . . It grew louder and louder . . . and we heard the rhythm of marching feet, the military rhythm of marching feet . . . the musical shuffle of the precise . . . left . . . right . . . left . . . right . . . the heartening sound of youthful marching feet . . . the murmur grew into a roar! . . . Down the boulevard came the familiar khaki . . . the broad sombreros of the American army! . . . PARIS WENT MAD!
—Peggy Hull, "The Last Crusade, 1918, A.D.," The Pointer

She paced the platform back and forth, waiting for the railroad to bring passengers from Kansas City to the east and Denver to the west. As trains came and went, she approached the travelers to ask for tidbits of news and gossip. Where had they been? Where were they going? What events were changing their lives? When the platform was empty and folks had gone their way, this girl reporter wrote up her findings and filed them with the editor of her small town newspaper, the *Junction City Sentinel*. The passengers might have noticed the ink stains on her fingers—not that she minded. Henrietta Eleanor Goodnough was plenty happy to typeset the articles she wrote.

Henrietta quit high school when she was 16, ready to do what it took to become a newspaper reporter. When she'd gleaned enough experience at home, she moved on. In two years' time, Henrietta lived in five states: Kansas, Colorado, California, Hawaii, and Minnesota. In Denver, she married George Hull, a newspaperman, and took his name. The marriage lasted only four years; Hull was a drunk, and when he stripped and tried to climb a flagpole naked (a fad that lasted long into the 1920s), Henrietta decided she'd had enough.

In Denver, Henrietta met and fell in love with another reporter, Harvey Duell. Harvey fell for Henrietta too; but he had his mother to think of, and she didn't approve of her son marrying a divorcée. Henrietta decided that absence might make Harvey's heart grow fonder, so true to style, she moved to Minnesota to work at the *Minneapolis Daily News*. There her editor insisted she change her name, saying he "wouldn't be caught dead putting at the head of any column in his newspaper a name such as Henrietta Goodnough Hull." Henrietta changed her name to Peggy. And when Harvey didn't propose and a better job appeared in Ohio, she moved to Cleveland.

In the course of her many jobs, Peggy had worked in both public relations and advertising. Reporters looked down on this kind of writing, but amid a growing market of department store shoppers, newspaper owners counted on advertising to sell papers. Women might not have the vote, but savvy editors hired them to write both ad copy and features from the "woman's angle."

Product placement was a typical component of these stories, and Peggy Hull, girl reporter, was assigned to write an advertising column at the Cleveland *Plain Dealer*. Peggy supposedly went "a-shopping" and made up stories featuring products and services her readers could buy in downtown Cleveland. Her copy was so good she was featured in a pair of trade magazines, *Editor & Publisher* and the *Journalist*, which explained that Peggy's chief stunt . . . is to "have things happen to her" as she puts it, in order make the interest keen. . . . An example of one of her "happenings" was to have herself held up by a masked bandit, which story was used to advertise a bank.

Though she blatantly sold advertising as real news, Peggy tacked disclaimers at the end of her columns, a "P.S." to clarify that prices and locations she mentioned were purely advertising. Readers didn't seem to mind, and she kept her bosses and their advertisers happy.

Peggy grew up near Fort Riley, Kansas, and had always idolized the soldier's life. When Cleveland became the first American city to sponsor a National Guard Training Course for Citizens, she signed up for its Women's Auxiliary. "I'm going to learn to shoot a rifle and to do Red Cross work," she wrote in the *Plain Dealer*. "The drills and exercise are splendid from a health standpoint, and the military training teaches self-control, a good thing for the majority of us because we are so apt to lose our heads in an emergency." She wrote a description of her uniform and went on to mention the frilly Easter outfit she'd wear off duty. Her Easter finery, of course, was available for purchase at a Cleveland store.

In 1916, Peggy began wearing a uniform full time. That year, the Mexican bandit Pancho Villa began a series of terrorist raids on American towns along the US-Mexican border, terrorizing and killing American citizens. On March 15, 1916, troops led by army general John J. Pershing were ordered to cross from Texas into Mexico to chase down Villa. The Ohio National Guard was sent to patrol the border, and Peggy decided to go along.

In true fashion, she got a head start. She boarded a train for El Paso, Texas, took a room in a hotel, and went to work as a freelancer. She had the *Plain Dealer's* promise to pay her for anything she wrote that could promote its advertisers. She stopped at home in Kansas on her way south. "Wherever the army was there was Peggy," the *El Paso Morning Times* said later. "When reviews [parades] were held at Fort Bliss, Peggy was there on the friskiest mount in the corrals. . . . When General Murgia [Mexican General Francisco Murgía] entertained General [J. Franklin] Bell in the hippodrome in Juarez toasts were drunk to Señorita Peggy, the pride of the Americans present. She was the friend of every soldier in the American army."

Peggy adored the pomp and circumstance of army life, but she wrote about its sordid side as well. As with all armies, Pershing's forces had its share of camp followers, prostitutes who found willing customers among the soldiers. In time, Peggy grew to understand the despair these scorned women shared, and when they were thrown out of town she wrote a sympathetic article about eight "little girls in red satin middy blouses . . . with a stigma that marks them 'undesirables.'"

Peggy joined 20,000 of Pershing's men on a 15-day march from Texas into New Mexico. She set off wide-eyed and excited, daydreaming of the entrance she'd make one day meeting an editor at the biggest New York newspaper, only to stumble over a rock and fall into a mesquite bush. The boots she'd bought hurt her feet so badly she fell behind and limped into camp with a pair of straggling soldiers. She was so sore the next morning she thought of turning back, until the sound of a bugle gave her the boost she needed.

Though the march was short that day, a sudden sandstorm created chaos all along the line of soldiers.

Units became separated. Minor commands were lost. Water wagons were overturned in the desert or else lost their way and wandered from the main column. The wind raged and blinded us all with fine white sand. We had no luncheon and no dinner. About 1 o'clock in the morning after the storm had spent itself, our weary field kitchen staggered into camp and the First Kentucky Field Hospital—I was traveling with them—turned out for food—and such food. Sanded bacon—sanded bread—sanded coffee sweetened with sanded sugar.

I felt as though I had never had a bath. . . . My hair was bristling and hard to sleep on. I didn't want a military career then, but I had convinced the general I did want one and I couldn't quit.

"Private" Peggy Hull was a tough young woman, and she hung on for four more days. She stood in chow lines with enlisted men to get her meals and slept on the ground in a small tent. Then, at the halfway point of the march, she was ordered to appear at the officers' mess tent. She'd received a "promotion," and as "Lieutenant Hull," Peggy was welcome to dine with the officers. Her toughness had won their admiration. What was more, Peggy Hull became the first American woman to "embed" with American forces, a term that didn't show up in the English language for another 80 years.

But Peggy's days with the *Plain Dealer* were numbered. There was only so much advertising a girl in Texas could sell for a department store in Cleveland, plus the paper had sent a male reporter to cover army news. When her editor asked her to come home, she sent her answer, which appeared in a feature article several years later:

"Won't come back; fire me if you like," she wired.

He did.

Plucky as ever, Peggy got a new job with the *El Paso Morning Times*. She decided to blend in with the men she covered and put together an outfit to wear in the field. Years later, her close friend, another newspaperwoman named Irene Corbally Kuhn, wrote about Peggy's days along the Texas-Mexican border:

> Peggy always dressed for the role. She wore a trim officer's tunic, short skirt, boots, Sam Browne belt [a wide leather belt with a strap that ran over the shoulder], and a campaign hat. She went right along on the marches with the boys, never complained that her feet hurt, nor interrupted things to powder her nose. Nighttime, she rolled up in her poncho and slept on the ground with the rest of them.

Peggy may have dressed to fit in, but the fact was that any girl reporter would cause a ruckus among thousands of soldiers. Even General Pershing knew her name. Peggy had ridden out to greet the general as he led his soldiers back from Mexico, and their picture ran the next day in the *Morning Times*. Pershing was not pleased to see himself upstaged by Peggy, whose place in the photo made it seem she'd led the parade.

War correspondents such as Peggy Hull wore uniforms to avoid being arrested as spies.
Spencer Research Library, University of Kansas Libraries

Nothing was going to stop Peggy Hull from getting a story. When the United States entered World War I in April 1917, the *Morning Times* agreed to sponsor her, provided that Peggy pay for her voyage and her expenses herself. If she were lucky enough to get some stories, then her editors would be happy to pay for them.

Peggy almost beat Pershing's soldiers to Paris, arriving just as the first troops from the American Expeditionary Force appeared. Unlike her male counterparts, who held credentials from the War Department, Peggy was completely on her own. She filed her early stories, How Peggy Got to Paris, with the El Paso paper, and they caught the eye of Floyd Gibbons, who reported for the *Chicago Tribune*. With Gibbons' approval, Peggy tweaked her words for the soldiers who read the *Tribune's* army edition. Always the innovator, Peggy offered her shopping services for the "boys" in the Expeditionary Force. She also found a friend in the older, elegant Anne McCormick, wife of an American businessman working abroad, who was to become a respected—and the first female—member of the *New York Times* editorial board after starting as a freelancer in Europe.

Peggy longed to get inside an army training site, but she lacked official credentials. Sympathetic officers managed to get her into an American artillery camp with a group of YMCA canteen workers, the only women besides nurses allowed anywhere near fighting men. She lived with the eight YMCA workers in a barracks heated by stoves and was up at 5:45 AM to wash her face in a basin of water and comb her hair in front of a tiny mirror. Peggy watched as soldiers learned how to fire trench mortars, which she likened to "gray devils" that could kill her if they went off course. When it came time to send the trainees to the battle line, Peggy rode 28 miles in the rain to see them off.

For the most part, male correspondents in France were slow to write war news. Waiting for the "real" fighting to start, they hadn't bothered with the human-interest stories that were Peggy's specialty. Peggy both entertained and informed the folks back home, and her woman's take on a soldier's life worked so well that other editors took notice and asked their reporters why they didn't produce the same stuff. The angry newsmen ganged up on Peggy, complaining to army brass that her work as an uncredentialed correspondent was "undignified." They forced the issue with Pershing, who admired Peggy and her gutsy reporting but refused to give her credentials.

Faced with leaving France, Peggy made plans to return to El Paso, where she was popular with the locals. When she departed, she made a dig at the men who'd forced her out of France.

When we've won the war and all you brilliant writers are out of jobs, come back to El Paso, Texas, and if you crowd my stuff off the front page there will still be two persons who'll look for it inside—mother and me. And I promise I won't fuss with the managing editor about it—or tell him you should be sent to Mexico or even ask him to put you in jail—I learned to be a good loser long before I came to France.

I cannot leave France without publicly announcing my gratitude and appreciation of the hospitality of Maj. Gen. Peyton C. March and his staff—of the YMCA men and women workers when my colleagues were seeking my blonde scalp . . .

Peggy went home but wasn't there for long. By the New Year in 1919, she was on the move and making headlines herself:

PEGGY HULL, NERVY WAR CORRESPONDENT, BRAVES SIBERIA'S TERRORS TO GET NEWS

—

First Covered Trains for Kansas
Paper; She Reported Movements
of Pershing's Army in Mexico and Then in France

—

She's Gathered News in Honolulu,
and Now She's in Far East in
Search of Facts About Mysterious
Russia and Siberia

The world war was over, but the Russian Revolution still raged, and Peggy made plans to report from Vladivostok. First she needed credentials; there was no way she could get all the way across the Pacific to eastern Russia without money and the all-important paperwork.

Her task didn't come easy. Peggy moved to Washington, DC, where she sent letters and telegrams to every editor she could name. She had to get approval from the army too and made an appointment with the very General March she'd known in France. Broader-minded than most men in his position (he was army chief of staff), March guaranteed he'd supply credentials to Peggy—*if* she could find an editor to pay her way to Siberia.

It took weeks to make a good connection until S. T. Hughes, editor in chief of the Newspaper Enterprise Association syndicate, reviewed Peggy's record and agreed to sponsor her. Armed with these pledges, she went to the Office of Military Intelligence to get her paperwork, but the captain in charge put her off. Peggy insisted she had official permission, and then he accused her of lying. Peggy left and returned in one hour with a stern directive from General March: "If your only reason for refusing Miss Peggy Hull credentials is because she is a woman, issue them at once and facilitate her procedure to Vladivostok." Peggy Hull had won her longed-for credentials, the first American woman to become an official war correspondent. A hometown paper printed the letter she wrote to her parents from Vladivostok on November 24, 10 days after she arrived from Japan on a filthy boat. Full of news and musing, the letter's tone was classic Peggy:

> I attended two dances while in Yokohama and met a number of Americans who have been living in the Far East for some time. The people stood around in groups watching me dance in uniform, and my various partners said they were all puzzled because I could manage to dance in my boots. I aroused a lot of curiosity in Japan because I was the first woman they had ever seen in uniform, and the Japanese men are very much opposed to their women doing anything but raise children, so they openly disapproved of me, which bothered me a whole lot you may well know. Fortunately there is an American hotel in Yokohama where one can have a private bath—the Japanese men and women bathe together, and in some parts you can't get a private bath.

Once she got to Vladivostok, Peggy had trouble finding a bathtub of any sort.

It was chaos in Siberia, where the Russian Revolution raged. The slaughter went on around her, as Bolsheviks and White Russians killed each other and wild bands of soldiers and bandits preyed on the innocent. Peggy's report ran in the *Cleveland Press* on March 6, 1919.

Siberia is on the threshold of its blackest period. Twice a victim first to monarchy and then to anarchy—its people this winter will die by thousands. They are freezing to death now and the coldest weather is still to come. Farther inland, where the disorganization of the railroads has made it impossible to carry supplies, they are starving to death, while roving bands of Bolsheviki and bandits terrorize the unprotected communities.

Murder, pillage, starvation, and bitter cold—what a desperate outlook.

Together with its allies, the US Army was quietly backing the White Russians in their battles against the Bolsheviks. Elements of the British and Japanese armies were in Siberia as well. The American mission was confusing because Allied generals couldn't determine exactly whom to support. Command and authority broke down, and many American soldiers took to the streets like punks, not the boys Peggy had so admired in Texas and France. When the Americans departed in June 1919, their commander, General William Graves, wrote that the US government had wrongly backed the White Russians,

a monarchistically inclined and unpopular Government, of which the great mass of the people did not approve. The United States gained, by this act, the resentment of more than 90 percent of the people of Siberia. . . .

I must admit, I do not know what the United States was trying to accomplish.

It was a thoroughly miserable experience, and the fact that Peggy's stories either went unpublished or were heavily edited didn't help. She also had her safety to consider. Vladivostok was filled with thieves and murderers. Windows were sealed shut to preserve the heat, and everything stank. Cafes were filthy, as were the people who cooked and served her meals. There wasn't a single bathtub where Peggy could get clean (General Graves would not permit her to use his), until a sympathetic navy admiral invited her to use the tub on his ship.

By summertime, all of the Allied nations began to ship their troops home from Siberia. Peggy rushed to leave Vladivostok and Siberia, a dirty and bitter place with a dark future. Siberia became a giant prison camp for millions of children, women, and men who stood against the Bolsheviks—later the Communists—who ruled Russia from 1919 until 1989.

As luck would have it, Peggy traveled through Shanghai, China, on her way home to the States. A port city, Shanghai hosted a large expatriate community of Americans and Europeans who made China their home. There she did two stints at the *Shanghai Gazette*, an English-language newspaper that was the mouthpiece for Sun Yat-sen, a Chinese reformer. Americans and Europeans lived in an area known as the Bund, an 8.3-square-mile area that sat along the Huangpu River. This "Paris of the East" attracted all manner of people who wanted to live a posh life on the cheap; a houseful of Chinese servants cost pennies in American dollars or British pounds.

But the real Paris called to Peggy as well, so in 1921 she moved there, thinking that her old friend Floyd Gibbons could find her a job. Peggy took a room in a cheap hotel where she met another reporter 10 years her junior, who was to become a lifelong friend. Her name was Irene Corbally, a Chicago girl hired by Gibbons as a fashion writer for the *Chicago Tribune*.

Just as quickly as she came, Peggy decided to leave Paris and return to Shanghai and her old job. On a whim—and angry at her boyfriend—Irene went along. Their adventures on the voyage from Marseilles across the Mediterranean, through the Suez Canal and on to Ceylon (now Sri Lanka) and Singapore could fill a book all by themselves. For Peggy, the highlight of the journey came when she boarded another ship in Singapore to look for an old friend, only to come across another acquaintance, a British officer named John Kinley. They promptly fell in love, and Peggy dropped her plan to sail on to China, trusting Irene to deal with her 11 suitcases in Shanghai.

Eventually Peggy and John Kinley set up housekeeping in Shanghai's International Settlement. It was a pampered life, but Peggy sensed the growing discontent among the Chinese who worked for the Europeans. Wages were down in the Bund, because a tidal wave of Russian refugees were happy to work for very low pay, undercutting and "breaking the rice bowls" of the Chinese. The insulted Chinese lost their high regard for their white employers, as general unrest against foreigners rippled across China.

As lovely as life was in the Bund, with its tea dances, diplomatic receptions, opera, and theater, Peggy warned that Western influence in China was in danger of yielding to Russian communism. "China is worth the struggle," she wrote, "but the Russians are going to get it, if you don't watch out!"

As much as her head governed her abilities as a newswoman, so had Peggy's heart led her into a second, ill-thought marriage. By the fall of 1925, she and John Kinley had separated, and Peggy came home to the United States only to discover that, by marrying a foreigner, she had lost her American citizenship and couldn't stay. She stalled for months longer than her temporary visa permitted, facing deportation as she petitioned US officials to change the rules. She went public with her predicament, and news of Peggy's "exile" was splashed in papers everywhere. It took five years before the immigration law was corrected by Congress, and by then, Harvey Duell had come back into her life. They decided to marry, but first Peggy had to return to Shanghai to get a divorce from John Kinley.

Peggy's trip in search of divorce papers turned into a blessing for her career. In January 1932, just as she got to China, Japan attacked Shanghai. "Go to work; you're our correspondent," cabled Harvey from his post with the *New York Daily News*. Peggy did, working 24-7 for three days straight; for a month she slept in an office chair. To scoop other reporters, she found someone with a short-wave radio to relay her stories across the Pacific in a quick 20 minutes; it took several hours before other correspondents could file theirs via cable. Equipped with notebook and field glasses, she watched as the Japanese sent air raids over Shanghai. At least once she climbed to the top of a flour mill, a serviceable but dangerous observation post to watch Japanese planes bomb a working-class neighborhood:

> The tenements crumbled like pie crusts and the ruins burst into flames as the terrified Chinese fled into the narrow streets, running in packs like bewildered animals. Thousands huddled in the debris. It was a frightful scene of human misery.

Shanghai endured the assault for six weeks before the Japanese withdrew. As a neutral observer, Peggy Hull was allowed to interview both Chinese and Japanese military leaders. She boarded a warship to interview Japanese admiral Kichisaburo Nomura and posed with him for a picture that ran in papers at home. Nomura, an honorable man, gifted Peggy with a safe conduct pass stamped on muslin to tuck in her purse.

On her way to interview a Chinese general, Peggy and her driver, a Russian veteran, mistakenly took a route directly into fighting between the Chinese and Japanese. Abandoning their car, they took refuge in a mound-shaped Chinese tomb, but not before Japanese soldiers spotted them. As the soldiers approached the tomb and fired, Peggy watched her driver, Sasha, with the "crazed fury of a trapped man," panic and run outside, where he was gunned down. From her hiding spot Peggy watched as "groups of short, stocky, khaki-clad, dark-skinned men bore down, their rifles smoking at exact intervals."

Grateful she wasn't wearing Chinese gray, Peggy dug into her purse but couldn't find the safe conduct pass. At first she panicked but then came to her senses when she remembered that the folded fabric was inside her passport. She stuck the pass on her coat with hairpins, fluffed up her hair to look as womanly as possible, emerged from the tomb, and raised her hands. The sight of a white woman surprised the Japanese, and for a moment, it crossed Peggy's mind that these men might be as afraid of dying as she was. A shocked Japanese officer sent her to his headquarters, where to her surprise Peggy met a general she had known in Vladivostok. "You know," he told her," if you do not give up your war corresponding, you are surely going to end your life on a battlefield."

Peggy returned to her Shanghai hotel as the assault dragged on. By the end of February, thousands of Chinese refugees had taken shelter in the International Settlement, and its Western residents were reacting oddly:

> In a seemingly endless stream they [the refugees] came trudging along, in the flapping blue cotton trousers and black coats, carrying bundles and babies on their backs, in their arms, and in creaking wheelbarrows and groaning carts.
>
> In vivid contrast to their anguish was the scene that was then being enacted within the ivory marble halls of

the Cathay Hotel, just 100 yards away. Under beautiful murals and amber lights, crowds of foreigners—their fears relieved by the failure of the Chinese artillery to respond to the Japanese attack—drank cocktails, sipped tea, and listened to splendid music.

That eerie display of denial showed up time and again in reports from war zones.

Peggy Hull eventually returned to New York, married Harvey Duell, and made her home with him until he died in 1939. During World War II she went back to work as a war correspondent, although it took two years for her to secure credentials. Peggy returned to the Pacific and won a navy commendation for her reporting as she moved from island to island. She talked with soldiers and sailors 30 years younger than she was, always in search of small but significant stories to share with readers. After the war, Peggy moved to California, where she died in 1967.

Historians compare Peggy Hull Duell with the legendary war reporter Ernie Pyle, who was killed by a Japanese sniper in the Pacific. Pyle's fame came during wartime. Scholars didn't recognize Peggy Hull's work until the 1980s, after women researchers rightly pointed out that "history" should include "her story," too.

The Russian Revolution

Russia was a gigantic but backward empire when it went to war against Germany in 1914. Russia's Industrial Revolution didn't come until 1890, more than a century after it came to Western Europe. When it arrived, Russian industry served the needs of the czar's autocratic government, and a prosperous middle class never arose as it had in the United States and Western Europe. What was more, unlike the monarchs in Western Europe, Czar Nicholas II, the last of the Romanov Dynasty, held real power. A revolution in 1906 had forced the czar to establish a Duma (parliament), but it had no true authority.

In the early spring of 1917, with the war going poorly and people hungry at home, citizens in the Russian capital of Petrograd (today St. Petersburg) surged into the streets to call for an end to the monarchy. The Russian military permitted the monarchy to collapse. Nicholas II abdicated the throne and was exiled with his family to Siberia. The Winter Palace in Petrograd, home to the czar's family, became the seat of Russia's new provisional government. The Winter Palace, a massive structure with hundreds of rooms, was to become the symbol of power during the weeks that followed.

However, competing political groups already had plans to force their own forms of government on Russia. The political situation changed almost weekly over the summer. At first, the Mensheviks, political moderates, seemed to have the upper hand. However, the radical Bolsheviks, under their leader, Vladimir Lenin, were building a grassroots insurgency. The Bolsheviks claimed to speak for Russia's vast, poor underclass—peasants, factory workers, and foot soldiers. In the October Revolution of 1917, the Bolsheviks seized the Winter Palace and overthrew the provisional government.

Lenin and his small inner group who made up the Communist Party consolidated their power across Russia in 1918. They allowed no dissent and murdered anyone who appeared to threaten them, including the deposed Czar Nicholas II and his wife, son, and four daughters. When the Communist Red Army was challenged by the moderate White Army, a vicious civil war spread across Russia from Petrograd in the west to Vladivostok in the east. Two years later, Lenin's Reds had gained control. The Communist Party ruled Russia (later renamed the Union of Soviet Socialist Republics) as a totalitarian government until 1989.

- -

Louise Bryant, Bessie Beatty, and Rheta Childe Dorr

- -

REPORTING FROM PETROGRAD

Whenever the firing dies down the correspondents used to make quick dashes into the streets to try to estimate the extent of the carnage, to count dead and dying men and horses lying on the pavements.—Rheta Childe Dorr

During the first critical months of the Russian Revolution in 1917, three American women journeyed to Petrograd to see the revolution for themselves. Each arrived with her own outlook and set of expectations, and each went home with her own view of what revolution meant for Russia.

Louise Bryant, 31, working for the Bell Syndicate and Philadelphia *Ledger*, accompanied her husband John Reed, a passionate communist and gifted writer who chronicled the Bolsheviks' rise to power. Bessie Beatty, at 30 a crusader for social justice, had covered miners' strikes in Nevada and written about the desolate lives of prostitutes in the *San Francisco Bulletin*. Americans knew Rheta Childe Dorr as the author of the syndicated column *As a Woman Sees It* for the *New York Daily Mail*. Nearly 50 and a veteran journalist, Rheta had made news herself as a suffragist when she challenged President Woodrow Wilson face-to-face during a White House meeting.

The three crossed paths reporting not only on the Russian Revolution, where Russians warred among themselves, but also during Russia's battles against Germany during the Great War. Americans wondered whether their Russian allies would keep their commitments as allies against Germany. With even more revolution brewing and so much at stake at home, would Russia's new, moderate government pull out of the war?

Newspapers all across the United States sent reporters to find out. Male correspondents were tasked with reporting on the war and Russian politics, the hard and fast news of emperors, governments, generals, battles, and casualties. Their dispatches were cabled home for immediate publication before the news grew stale.

Matters were different for Louise Bryant, Bessie Beatty, and Rheta Dorr, the only three American women reporters who got to Petrograd and Moscow during World War I. Their job was to report on the "women's angle" of war and revolution to draw women readers, but their stories often appeared weeks after they were written. Editors didn't rush them into print in the same way they handled hard news filed by men. Bessie Beatty's eyewitness account of the fall of the Winter Palace bore a December 1, 1917, dateline, but the San Francisco Bulletin didn't print it until January 28, 1918. Her woman's observations lacked the same standing as a man's reporting.

But reading their reports dropped Americans right into the drama in Petrograd. Louise, Bessie, and Rheta wrote in first person, almost as if they were creating memoirs. Their stories drew readers across time and space to that remote and strange Russia: Bessie and Louise sidestepping mobs as they fought in the streets; Rheta taking tea in a convent with a Romanov grand duchess turned mother superior (the Bolsheviks later murdered her); Bessie dancing the mazurka with a Russian officer in a small village.

All three correspondents knew fear and understood the risks. Rheta lay in her hotel bed one night listening as a gang of Bolshevik sympathizers slaughtered an old general in the next room. Louise put herself in danger by going to Moscow to witness a Red Funeral, when the Bolshevik revolutionaries laid their dead to rest in red-stained coffins inside the Kremlin wall. Bessie, as she did her interviews all across Petrograd, witnessed scores of killings, sometimes of soldiers, others of innocent onlookers. She could have been one of them.

Bessie was the first into Petrograd, arriving via a convoluted route from the East. The *Bulletin* had sent her on assignment to report from Japan and China, and Bessie had been on board four days when word arrived that the United States had entered World War I. Bessie switched her destination to Petrograd by heading north to Vladivostok, Russia, where she embarked on a 12-day train trip across Russia, riding from the Pacific Ocean to the Baltic Sea some 6,000 miles west. When the Trans-Siberian Express, the "train deluxe of the longest railroad in the world" arrived in the middle of the night, no one was waiting for its weary passengers, the first hint that life in Petrograd was changing.

When Bessie first walked its streets in June 1917, Petrograd, a Russian jewel, was abloom with flowers. Russia was in the hands of a provisional government, and the scene seemed peaceful. Bessie watched a young couple stroll through a park, tagging them with the names "Vera" and "Ivan."

Peace, joy, exultation, was upon that spring-clad city. Freedom was young then, like the spring, like the leaves on the trees, like Vera and Ivan. . . .

Poor Ivan! Poor Vera! They could not guess that afternoon, any more than I, what the months would do to their butterfly treasure. They could not know that they themselves would soon lay violent hands upon it. . . .

Russia was descending into chaos. War with Germany already had placed huge demands on its people. With Russia's old class system abolished and everything from factories to farms to schools to the police organized into soviets—committees of ordinary citizens—Russian society fell into disorder. Crops rotted in railway cars; soldiers refused to salute their officers and deserted the army. With no one to operate machinery, factory production ground to a halt. Bessie noticed the queues, lines that formed everywhere in Petrograd for bread, kerosene, shoes, chocolate, and even shipping trunks for those who hoped to escape Russia forever. Louise ached for the hungry children she saw throughout the countryside. Rheta wrote that 90 percent of Russians could not read and asked how such hungry, uneducated, and fatalistic people could establish a sane democracy.

Week by week, Bessie Beatty, Louise Bryant, and Rheta Dorr mingled with the mighty and the masses as the summer and fall of 1917 unfolded. Bessie and her interpreter rode trains to the battle zone, scrounging seats as best they could in a new Russia where there was no longer such a thing as a reservation for a sleeping berth—for the moment, the revolution meant first come, first served.

Bessie's successful journey to the battle zone made her the only American woman to get to the Eastern Front in World War I. Standing just 160 feet from the trenches, she gazed from an observation post across no-man's-land, "like a bone between two hungry dogs," at the Russian-German line. As she stood with a Russian officer and her interpreter taking in the scene, she thought she saw something move.

> Suddenly my wandering mind stopped short. Two black specks appeared for a moment above that metal line. On the instant two rifles cracked—short, sharp, and final. The specks were gone. I caught my breath. It could not be true! I had imagined it.
>
> The officer beside me was speaking. I had not heard. I begged his pardon abstractedly, and he repeated:
>
> "A couple of Germans put their heads over the trench—bad thing to do."

More unusual were the reports coming from Russia that women were in combat fighting the Germans. Bessie Beatty and Rheta Childe Dorr traveled together to training camps to confirm these bizarre rumors. Yes, these raw

Bessie Beatty (left) and Louise Bryant posed with a Russian count who served as a military commandant.
Courtesy of the Family of Bessie Beatty and the Occidental College Special Collections and College Archives

soldiers were women, volunteers who planned to relieve their exhausted men at the Eastern Front, many of whom had deserted the army. They called themselves the Battalion of Death, led by a rough peasant named Maria Bachkarova (today spelled Bochkareva). Bessie and Rheta slept in the wooden barracks that were home to this motley crew. Every night they rolled themselves into brown blankets and shared a sleeping platform with Bochkareva and her aide, an educated girl named Marya Skridlova. All it did was rain, so the women drilled inside counting "Ras dva tri chetiri ras dva tri chetiri" ("One two three four one two three four") for hours on end.

In July 1917, Bessie and Rheta spent a week living with these women, who had shaved their heads and donned men's boots to go to war. They sidestepped laundry, boots, and gas masks hanging from rafters in their barracks and shared the soldiers' rations of black bread and soup. The women were of every class and type, rough girls from the country and demoiselles from the city.

Every "soldier girl" had a story to tell, and Bessie pieced together what "pushed them out of their individual ruts into the mad maelstrom of war." One was an orphan, another a secretary, yet another a Polish refugee who had fled from the German army. One was Japanese. One of them kissed her rifle as thought it were her lover. "I love my gun," she told Bessie. "It carries death. I love my bayonet too. I love all arms. I love all things that carry death to the enemies of my country."

Then came the call everyone was waiting for: the Women's Battalion was going into battle. Bessie and Rheta went back to Petrograd; Rheta felt it wasn't right for her to follow the women into battle because she would "simply have been a nuisance." Both Rheta and Bessie wrote long articles about the women and the aftermath of battle. The women soldiers, the reporters said, conducted themselves with honor. Bessie's words rang with drama:

> All the world knows how they went into battle shouting a challenge to the deserting Russian troops. All the world knows that six of them stayed behind in the forest, with wooden crosses to mark their soldier graves. Ten were decorated for bravery in action with the Order of St. George, and 20 others received medals. Twenty-one were seriously wounded, and many more than that received contusions. Only fifty remained to take their places with the men in the trenches when the battle was over. . . .
>
> I heard the story from the lips of twenty of the wounded women. No one of them can tell exactly what happened.
>
> "We were carried away in the madness of the moment," one of them said. "It was all so strange and exciting; we had no time to think about being afraid."
>
> "No," said Marya Skridlova. "I was not afraid. None of us were afraid. We expected to die, so we had nothing to fear."
>
> Then the demoiselle came to the surface again. "It was hard, though. I have a cousin—he is Russian in his heart, but his father is a German citizen. He was drafted: he had to go. When I saw the Germans, I thought of him. Suppose I should kill him? Yes, it is hard for a woman to fight."

Marya Skridlova got her Cross of St. George, and she came back to Petrograd walking with a limp as a result of shell shock.

"There were wounded Germans in a hut," she said. "We were ordered to take them prisoners. They refused to be taken. We had to throw hand-grenades in and destroy them. No; war is not easy for a woman."

Bessie Beatty, Louise Bryant, and John Reed were in Petrograd to witness the October Revolution, the turning point in that fateful autumn of 1917, when the Bolsheviks stormed the Winter Palace, threw out Russia's provisional government, and set up a government under Lenin. On the night of October 24–25, 1917, Bessie wangled a valuable pass bearing the blue seal of the Bolshevik Military Revolutionary Committee. The reporters depended on their passes to keep them out of trouble with bands of Red Guards ("factory men with rifles") on the lookout for "bourgeoisie"—enemies of the revolution.

The three Americans climbed into a truck that was dropping Bolshevik leaflets throughout Petrograd. (Louise was asked to remove the yellow band from her hat; it was an attractive target for snipers.) Meeting roadblocks and showing their passes when challenged, they finally arrived at the Winter Palace to stand in the shadow of a "great red arch." The boom of a big gun and the crack of rifle fire echoed across the square where they watched as Red fighters, armed with guns and bayonets, stormed the palace.

And then it was all over. Louise and Bessie remarked how little looting went on in the lavish palace that first night when the Bolsheviks captured it. Their observations were soon challenged by other newsmen who charged the Bolsheviks with stripping the palace bare of its valuable art and sculpture, destroying much of it furnishings, rugs, and china. Louise believed that wagonloads of priceless treasures had left the palace for Moscow well before the Bolsheviks took it, broadly hinting that the precious cargo was in Moscow for safekeeping in case Petrograd was invaded by the German army.

Louise Bryant insisted that the Bolsheviks weren't nearly as violent as some claimed; she wrote that she could "go about" in a fur coat with no problems, and that theaters, the ballet, and movies still drew audiences.

It is silly to defend the revolution by claiming there has been no bloodshed and it is just as silly to insist that the streets are running blood. No one can predict what will happen before the problem of a new government is settled in Russia, but up to the present moment the actions of the mass, so long mistreated and suppressed, and now suddenly given liberty has been surprisingly gentle.

With their strong support for the rights of oppressed working men and women, Bryant and Beatty hoped that the Bolsheviks, who claimed to represent the working classes, would create a just and lasting society that valued everyone. "To have failed to see the hope in the Russian Revolution is to be as a blind man looking at a sunrise," Bessie wrote in what was to become one of her best-known lines.

But Rheta Childe Dorr, an avowed progressive who had exposed the shameful working conditions in American factories, left Petrograd with grave doubts about the fate of Russia's working poor.

I saw a people delivered from one class tyranny deliberately hasten to establish another, quite as brutal and as unmindful of the common good as the old one. . . . I saw a working class which had been oppressed under czardom itself turn oppressor; an army that had been starved and betrayed use its freedom to starve and betray its own people. I saw elected delegates to the people's councils turn into sneak thieves and looters. I saw law and order and decency and all regard for human life or human rights set aside.

Each with her own impressions in mind, Louise Bryant, Bessie Beatty, and Rheta Childe Dorr rushed home to write their books. Louise dedicated *Six Red Months in Russia* to her husband, "that beloved vagabond John Reed." Bessie compiled her articles into *The Red Heart of Russia*, published in 1918.

Rheta Childe Dorr returned home note-free and wrote completely from memory. "[I] had not dared to write a line while I was in Russia," she wrote later in her autobiography, *A Woman of Fifty*. "I sat at my typewriter hour after hour, oblivious to my surroundings, and when I got up from the day's work I was always astonished not to see from the window roofs of Petrograd or

the domed churches the Kremlin. When it was all over I felt like an emptied pitcher."

Rheta Childe Dorr.
Library of Congress
mnwp 15000

Rheta Childe Dorr went back to Europe as a war reporter, but French authorities refused her pleas for credentials. Wise to the fact that women "had learned through uncounted centuries to move by indirection," she end-ran the French by signing up with the YMCA as an entertainer. She couldn't sing or dance, so she entertained the troops by giving lectures about the Russian Revolution. There was a bonus: Rheta hoped to see her son Julian, who was serving in France. She met the top man himself, General John Pershing, who "seemed amused at the spectacle of a war mother going around France in riding breeches and a service cap." Rheta delivered her lectures, got her stories, and saw her son twice. She continued to write books, including a biography of Susan B. Anthony. Her health began to fail after her son died young in 1936, and she died in 1948 after many years of illness.

Louise Bryant attended another Red Funeral in 1922 when her husband John Reed died of typhus and was buried in the Kremlin, the only American to be so honored by the Bolsheviks. Louise picked up the pieces of her life and continued to work in the United States and Europe. She had a daughter, Anne, by her second husband, William Bullitt; but the marriage was unhappy, and Louise became estranged from her child. As the years moved on, her addiction to alcohol and drugs ruled her life. She died forgotten and alone in Paris in 1936.

Bessie Beatty became editor of *McCall's* magazine following her work in Russia. She stayed active in American journalism, wrote for Hollywood and the stage, and hosted a popular radio program on WOR Radio in New York. In 1942, *Time* called her "Mrs. Know It All," saying, "Her fans include the well-heeled and hard-up in almost equal numbers. They also include men. Yelled a bartender recently, when customers switched off Bessie's program: 'Don't youse guys want to learn nothing? You listen to Bessie Beatty. She'll teach you something.'" She died in 1947.

Today, the works of Bryant, Beatty, and Dorr are largely forgotten, as they were forgotten rather soon after World War I ended. When women requested press credentials to work as correspondents during World War II, they had to dig deep to discover that others had gone before them, 20 years earlier.

Helen Johns Kirtland

REPORTING FROM FRANCE

Mrs. Kirtland is the first and only woman correspondent to be allowed at the front since the famous Caporetto, at first as the guest of the navy and later of the army. Mrs. Kirtland photographed these troops under a late afternoon sun as they swung down the long road on their way to the lines.
      —*Leslie's Photographic Review of the Great War*

On November 15, 1917, the *New York Times* splashed wedding news on page 13. The granddaughter of the legendary banker J. P. Morgan had wed in a small and elegant but subdued ceremony "owing to the war." Below ran news of another wedding the day before:

BRIDE OF L. S. KIRTLAND.

The marriage of Miss Helen Warner Johns, daughter of Mrs. Henry Ward Johns of Lawrence Park, Bronxville, and Lucian Swift Kirtland of this city and Minneapolis,

Minn., was solemnized yesterday in Christ Church, Bronxville. The ceremony was performed by the Rev. Dr. Villson, rector of the church, assisted by the Rev. Mr. Robinson.

The bride wore a gown of white satin and old point lace. Her sister, Miss Mabel Johns, was maid of honor, and appeared in a frock of orchid-colored satin and net. The bridesmaids, the Misses Julia Warner, Emily Poucher, Janet Hayward, and Vivian Maxwell, wore pastel shades of green and sand. Albert Strong was best man. A reception followed at the home of the bride's mother.

Mr. Kirtland is a Yale graduate, class of 1903, and he and his bride will spend the winter in France.

If ever there were an understated mention of a honeymoon destination, it was in that wedding announcement. Helen and Lucien's "winter in France" was in truth a working honeymoon. Staff correspondents for *Leslie's Illustrated Weekly* magazine, Helen and Lucien were off to France to cover the war. As a man, Lucien had no trouble gaining credentials that gave him access to the front lines in France, but for Helen, the same rules didn't apply. The only American women in France were nurses, YMCA canteen workers and entertainers, and the special group of "Hello Girls" who worked as telephone operators at American headquarters. Not one woman was a credentialed war correspondent in the fall of 1917.

That didn't stop Helen. She wangled access to the front by somehow getting herself associated with the YMCA. That task accomplished and camera equipment in hand, she tramped all over France and Italy with her new husband.

No newcomer to European life, Helen was a veteran traveler when she accompanied Lucien to France. Her father, Henry

Photographer Helen Johns Kirtland posed with an exploded marine mine on the Belgian coast during World War I.
Library of Congress LC-DIG-ppmsca-32779

Johns, was a self-made man who invented and patented fireproof roofing shingles, getting his start in the basement of a New York tenement home where he experimented with his idea by pouring hot tar over old sheets and running them through a washing machine ringer.

Henry Johns died in 1898 of lung disease unwittingly brought on by the asbestos he used to make his products fireproof. Helen's mother Emily moved her two daughters to Bronxville, New York, a thriving art colony and home to writers, painters, and architects, and Helen grew up appreciating the visual arts. Her mother toured Europe with her girls, and decorative postcards they sent back and forth mentioned they were using cameras to "try some photos."

It's not clear how Helen Warner Johns met Lucien Kirtland, but they may have first crossed paths while working for *Leslie's* magazine. When the couple first arrived in France in the fall of 1917, most American forces will still in training and just beginning to arrive in Paris, just in time to relieve the exhausted

French and British armies who had been fighting Germany for
three long years.

Helen's photographs showed her skill with the big box camera that she took everywhere. She shot memorable images of
the bombed-out city of Verdun, France, from a ruined window
in a cathedral, Italian soldiers on the march, and French women
cutting and sewing the linen to cover the skeletons of rebuilt
Liberty planes.

One of the *Leslie's* articles stated that Helen was the only
woman permitted at the Italian Front after the disastrous Battle
of Caporetto, with 10,000 soldiers killed, 20,000 wounded, and
275,000 made captive by their Austrian enemies. Helen and Lucien also recorded the famed day of June 28, 1919, when the Treaty
of Versailles was signed in France and brought peace—for a
time—to Europe. But there was still the grinding, dangerous task
of clearing the countryside of unexploded armaments. Helen's
vivid description arrived on a postcard she sent to her mother:

> I am first beginning to get over the queer sensation of
> crossing the lines & wandering in no man's land, even yet
> one hears tremendous explosions now & then—& these
> only add local color—Appropriate sounds to describe the
> sights! For they are of course cleaning up the country of
> duds as systematically as they can—My! What a job!! I'd
> hate to be a farmer in these parts! . . . Every now & again
> someone gets "Bumped off."
>
> The shells & their little brothers the hand grenades,
> are not a race of savages to get too chummy with & stub
> your toe on one as you tramp thru the pits & hummocks
> among the lines—may mean—you won't finish the day's
> program. I am quite well trained—in fact I guess most of
> us who have been here during the war when the air was

alive with them, are & no souvenir hunting is worth risking the consequences of touching these steel fiends that may not be dead but only sleeping!

Leslie's Illustrated Weekly Newspaper credited Helen Johns Kirtland with photos she took at the Italian Front.
Library of Congress, LC-DIG-ppmsca-07628

The beaches too will have to undergo a spring clean-
ing to be ready for children & their sand pails & shovels
for they are chuck-full of barbed wire—& mines lie in
half dozens unexploded & menacing; some nearly buried
in drifts trying to sink into oblivion—to forget their era
& wicked life—others standing quite on tiptoe & ready to
fight—& when the wind blew sand around their "horns"
I imagined I could see smoke, warning us that given
occasion, or un-careful treatment, this round, fat dragon
would belch forth more than smoke—fire, sharp steel, &
destruction. One doesn't turn these things over on their
backs to see the other side!

After the war Helen and Lucien Kirtland traveled the globe as
Lucien wrote for a number of American magazines and penned
two books about Asia. Helen apparently worked in tandem with
Lucien taking pictures to accompany his articles, but her name
rarely appeared in credits. In one issue of *Leslie's Photographic
Review of the Great War*, however, she penciled in her initials,
H.J.K., next to an uncredited photo that apparently was hers.

The Kirtlands collected scores of art objects in their travels,
many of which were sold by an exclusive auction house after
Helen died in 1979. The couple had no children. The Library of
Congress holds a large collection of their photos, donated by a
family associate. Historians hope to dig deeper into Helen's life,
but the Kirtlands' books, letters, and other papers seem to have
disappeared without a trace.

2

Between
World Wars
1920–1939

With the armistice signed, Americans sailed home in 1919. They were greeted by a shaky economy, joblessness, and a gripping fear of communism in Russia and whether American workers would rise up in revolution. Shipyard strikes, steelworkers' riots, hints of Bolshevik teachings at colleges, and random bombings terrorized Americans. For a year this Red Scare dominated the headlines.

Americans, weary of foreign entanglements, yearned to settle back and forget the world's problems. In a landslide election in 1920, they sent Republican candidate Warren G. Harding to the White House. Harding promised a return to "normalcy," and back to normalcy Americans went. Armed with a tool called "credit," they spent their way into a booming economy. The good times rolled, and the stock market climbed ever higher.

So did hems on ladies' skirts. Trendy young women bound their breasts to fit into straight-up-and-down chemises. The bolder ones smoked in public, and the boldest chose to have sex outside of marriage.

Dailies and magazines still provided Americans with most of their news, and in 1920, KDKA in Pittsburgh, Pennsylvania, made radio's first commercial broadcast to announce that Harding had won the election. When people went to the movies, they viewed black-and-white newsreels with news from home and overseas.

Women continued working as journalists, but the social changes after World War I, including the right to vote, didn't change their status on newspaper staffs. Editors continued to assign their "girl reporters" to the "woman's angle," even at the new English-language papers in Europe. But that didn't stop young women with a nose for news from heading overseas.

London, Paris, and Berlin played host to American news agencies, and these young women, armed with college degrees, a bit of cash, and adventurous spirits, freelanced for the International News Service (INS), Associated Press (AP), and United Press (now known as UPI, United Press International). Placing one's articles with this or that wire service was a surefire way to get noticed and, with luck, find a paying job. Paris especially drew young Americans with a taste for adventure. Artists, musicians, poets, authors, booksellers, and newspaper reporters flocked to the City of Light. Rents were low, and wine was cheap.

From Indianapolis, Indiana, by way of New York came Janet Flanner, an aspiring poet and novelist who divorced her husband and embarked with her lover, Solita Solano, to Paris. Flanner, taking the pen name Genêt (which sounded like her first name), tantalized readers of the *New Yorker* magazine with

French gossip and tales of bohemian life. Anne O'Hare McCormick pitched stories to the *New York Times* and scored a telling interview with the young fascist Benito Mussolini when others ignored him.

Peggy Hull, fresh from months covering the Russian Revolution, moved to Paris and made a new friend in Irene Corbally, a girl from Greenwich Village, New York, who worked for the *Chicago Tribune*. Dorothy Thompson, a minister's daughter, got tired of her tame existence as a paid reformer and publicist and sailed to London in search of a newspaper job.

Hull and Corbally ended up circling the globe to work in China, while Thompson aimed her sights at the German-speaking nations. Another American reporter, the German-speaking Sigrid Schultz, was working in Berlin when Thompson first arrived.

Hull, Kuhn, Thompson, and Schultz were expected to write stories catering to female readers. However, they wrote what they saw, convinced that the United States could never maintain its isolationism, and they sent early warning signals about murderous governments in Germany and Asia that would drag Americans into World War II.

China, 1920–1939

After the fall of China's Qing Dynasty in 1911 there were hopes that a Chinese republic would replace it with the support of China's Nationalist Party. However, the notion of democracy in China failed as China's generals and warlords competed for power and built their own fiefdoms across the land. For China's millions of peasants, life didn't change; they continued to work the earth by hand as they had for centuries. In China's isolated cities, the poor lived in wretched conditions, many of them in the streets. There was next to no indoor plumbing or sewage treatment; human excrement was removed by laborers. (Westerners called them "night soil coolies." "Coolie" was a term for a person who did manual labor). Diseases such as cholera ran rampant. Beggars were a common sight. Women had no rights; frequently poor girls were sold by their families when they couldn't feed them. No national form of education existed, and just a handful of Chinese children went to school, often run by Christian missionaries.

But change was coming. The rise of a New Culture Movement offered elite young men university educations that exposed them to Western ideas such as the concept of democracy and the scientific method. The Soviet Union also sent advisors to assist the Nationalist Party and its leader Sun Yat-sen. For a time, the Nationalists joined forces with China's Communist Party, hoping to establish a republic across China.

In 1925 Sun Yat-sen died unexpectedly. His military commander, Chiang Kai-shek, took control of the Nationalists and marched north and successfully attacked several enemy warlords. Then in 1927, Chiang reversed course and attacked the Communists in his own party, murdering hundreds of Shanghai workers who had joined the Communists. In 1928 Chiang's army swept into China's capital, Beijing, consolidating power across China for the first time in 12 years. However, the Communist Party held on in widespread pockets across central and southern China. In 1934 Chiang's armies began to force the Communists out in a massive retreat known as the Long March during which hundreds of thousands of Communists died. Out of this debacle rose a new Communist leader, Mao Tse-tung (Mao Zedong) and his bright-minded associate Chou En-Lai.

Irene Corbally Kuhn

REPORTING FROM SHANGHAI

Turn the calendar back, give me another chance, and I'd do it all over again; nor would I take a million dollars cold for the experience. I wouldn't give up one heartache or trade any part of the agony or high adventure for a chance to live my life again in security and peace. To live close to reality is really to live.

—Irene Corbally Kuhn

In the summer of 1911, a teenage girl opened a book and wrote her signature on the flyleaf. Under her name and the date, she added an extra flourish as if to say, "I own this book and everything it stands for." *The Motor Boys in the Clouds, or, A Trip for Fame and Fortune* was new in bookshops, one of a series that took readers on colorful adventures as their characters battled to uphold what was right and just. Just seven years earlier, the Wright Brothers had made the first flight in an airplane, and publishers eagerly printed books for boys, hoping to score profits during those exciting times.

Of course, girls like this book's owner, one Irene A. Corbally of Greenwich Village, New York, enjoyed these stories too. A girl could dream, even if she couldn't look forward to doing everything that boys could. But Irene was determined to live out her dreams, and at 16, she left the path taken by most of the girls who lived in the small homes in Greenwich Village.

The girls and boys had spacious parks in which to play, and in those parks were trees as old as Manhattan Island, trees

under which they sat and held hands on green-painted benches while they "kept company." Few girls went to business; they graduated from school to helping around the house, learning to be housekeepers themselves for the neighborhood boys they were sure to marry.
Everybody thought I was a strange kind of girl because I turned up my nose at early marriage to a boy I had known all my life. I wanted to write and I wanted to travel.

Like so many Americans in the early 20th century, Corbally lived in a big household with her mother and grandparents and uncles and aunts, but it was her grandfather—with her grandmother's input—who ruled their Irish-American clan. At 16, Irene announced that she was leaving high school to train as a stenographer, and her grandfather challenged her.

Irene explained that working would allow her to meet people, learn about life, and become a writer. A job as a stenographer could be the first step toward landing a job at a magazine or newspaper. Irene knew enough about herself to realize that she wasn't a writing genius; she would need to practice. She saw herself as one of the "craftsmen who learned to write by putting down one word after another until they could do it with their eyes closed."

Irene's grandfather granted her wish and sent her to a seven-month stenography school to learn shorthand and typing. She went to work, moving from job to job but always making sure that each one paid a little bit more. As soon as she got work typing letters at *Collier's*, a popular national magazine, she was sure she'd worm her way into a writing job. That didn't happen, and, disappointed, Irene realized that the "ink-stained company I wanted to join were still far beyond my reach."

Irene went to work as secretary to a Columbia University scientist, who did experiments all day and wrote them up all night. Dr. William J. Gies, professor of biological chemistry, added Irene to his research team studying salvarsan, a German drug that promised to combat the effects of syphilis, the deadly sexually transmitted infection that scourged young American soldiers who were at war in France. Dr. Gies respected his secretary's intelligence, and he taught her how to take measure of herself in both her personal and professional life.

Irene started college classes at Marymount College, but she didn't fit in with girls who were younger and not as worldly. Dr. Gies suggested she enroll at Columbia in its Extension Department, and Irene became an early example of a nontraditional student with a pile of textbooks in contemporary literature, French, logic, philosophy, modern European history, and some writing courses. When she felt ready to look for a job in New York City, the nation's publishing hub, an old-time newspaperman suggested she first get experience upstate.

Irene found a job at the *Syracuse Herald*, which paid $18 per week (less than $250 a week in today's dollars). Working for the paper's city editor, Tom Powers, she quickly proved she had the "nose for news" that marked a successful reporter. Like other women working for newspapers, she was assigned to write feature stories with a "woman's angle." She yearned for the day when she'd have a byline, usually reserved for hard news stories that appeared on the *Herald's* all-important front page. Her opportunity came when her brief but biting review of a movie caught her editor's fancy, and he gave her a byline. Soon Irene was writing a "short, bright" piece every day as she went around town to discover what people were talking about.

Equipped with upstate experience, Irene moved to the *New York Daily News*. Brainchild of the *Chicago Tribune*, the *News* grabbed readers who shied away from the content-heavy, solemn pages of the *New York Herald Tribune* or the *New York Times.* The *Daily News* was a "picture paper" tabloid called "the stenographer's delight and the gum chewer's dream." Human-interest stories featuring high adventure, cops and bootleggers, handsome heroes, and fallen women—these were the grist of tabloids such as the *Daily News.* If Americans needed newspapers to help them forget the horror of the Great War, then the tabloids were just the ticket.

But Irene, a woman, was forbidden to venture out to report on crime scenes and gangland shootings. Again she was assigned the women's angle, which, in tabloid reporting, meant stories about sex. Readers devoured them. In America's bigger cities, Irene noted,

> The war was over. The dead were buried. Most of the living had come home. Come home with a new philosophy gained from intimate acquaintance with trench living on borrowed time. Men had lived with death so long that they seized upon life with a rapist's lust, and life meant women and women meant sex.

Irene, caught up in the excitement of working at an energetic young newspaper, thrived as she wrote stories of scandal and shame. Readers gobbled them up. If Irene's editor, Phil Payne, came under fire for running too many questionable stories, she could argue that he was mirroring contemporary life.

But the *Daily News* wasn't selling enough papers, and Irene, last hired, was first fired. She found a new job as an advertising copywriter for a successful entrepreneur who was doing business in Paris. Her horse-faced, garishly dressed employer, who made millions selling patent medicines and cheap makeup, turned out to be a glorified snake-oil salesman. When she tried several times to correct glaring errors in ad proofs, she was ordered to be "grammatical someplace else." It soon dawned on Irene that she'd been hired for less-than-honorable reasons. Sure that she could take care of herself, she set sail for Paris.

From her seat in her Paris office, Irene watched male bosses hire and fire a round of "new pert French faces in the stenographic department to replace those which had been new and pert only a day or two before. . . . Today's favorite was tomorrow's candidate for the guillotine." One day, when it was clear to her bosses that she wasn't going to bed with them, she was fired.

But Irene had planned ahead. She held an all-important letter of introduction to Floyd Gibbons, who ran the *Chicago Tribune* Paris edition. Reporters worked in a space rented from a French paper, typing their stories on wooden boards nailed onto supports. A board table served as the copy desk, peppered with marks, "scorched reminders of smoldering cigarettes forgotten while tardy genius rang the typewriter bell."

Again assigned to write for women readers, Irene covered social events, fashion trends, and visits by famous Americans that included a stroll through the park with silent-movie genius Charlie Chaplin, as well as America's sweetheart, movie star Mary Pickford and her new husband, the dashing Douglas Fairbanks. When work hours got long and the *Tribune's* reporters grew thirsty, they lowered an empty pail from their courtyard window to be filled with beer by a café across the way. "We became so expert," Irene recalled, "we scarcely disturbed the foam. Never did beer taste so good."

Irene's assignments could turn serious. There was so much suffering in the world. She attended Memorial Day ceremonies outside Paris and gazed across fresh young grass at a field of white crosses decorated with little American flags. It was her job to check with the American Red Cross each day as it tracked the burials of more than 6,300 dead American soldiers and sent photos of their graves home to their families. When Floyd Gibbons flew into Russia as the first American eyewitness to a hideous famine, Irene's stomach did flip-flops as she translated Gibbons' "graphically ghastly" cable-ese—a style of telegraph shorthand that kept costs in check.

The next December, overtaken with restlessness and angry at her boyfriend, Irene sailed to China with her best pal, Peggy Hull, who had made a name for herself as America's only woman credentialed as a war correspondent. Peggy had been to Asia and was yearning get back. After a weeks-long trip on a Japanese freighter, whose crew assumed that Irene and Peggy were either loose women or spies, Irene arrived in Shanghai minus Peggy but with all of their luggage. During their voyage, Peggy had stumbled upon an old acquaintance, a British officer, and had eloped with him.

Irene had $25 in American Express checks and a letter of introduction that snagged her a job working for the English-language *China News*, whose Mesopotamian (Iraqi) owner had gone legit after successfully dealing in opium, Asia's drug of choice. On her first day at work, she joined her coworkers at a wedding reception, and there she met the love of her life, another *News* reporter named Bert Kuhn. Within weeks, Irene, who had dated many young men over the years, married Bert, left her job, and started to learn the elaborate ritual of home-making in China. They lived in the Bund, Shanghai's sector for Westerners, whose buildings reminded everyone of a German city. Irene looked back on those early days of marriage in a feature article she wrote for the *Los Angeles Times* in 1986, 40 years later:

Irene Corbally Kuhn hammed it up for her picture when she lived and worked in China. *Irene Kuhn Papers, American Heritage Center, University of Wyoming*

The standard requirements of a small household of a Westerner then consisted of a No. 1 Boy, a No. 1 Cook (and, if there was to be a lot of entertaining, a Small Cook as well), a Wash Amah, a gardener, a coolie and a jinriki-sha (. . . rickshaw) coolie, who came complete with his vehicle. That was the minimum. The place of the No. 1 Boy, I soon discovered, corresponded to that of the butler in a large English household. He served as general fac-totum, ran the rest of the staff and had certain specific additional duties such as serving drinks, waiting table and answering the door. He consulted with "Missy" daily for his marching orders, and he was charged with keep-ing the household books. At the end of every month there would be a reckoning with "Missy"; she would pay the No. 1 Boy, and he in turn would pay the suppliers. . . . He also collected a small slice of the wages of each of the servants under him in the household. There was never any protest or complaint, because it was all part of a complex code. More important, it worked.

In a short time Irene was pregnant, and she and Bert moved to Hawaii so their baby could be born in an American territory. Shanghai was no place to give birth—it was crowded with traffic, noise, and corruption. Even its professional beggars split their takings with a man who operated like some kind of union boss. Everywhere she looked, Irene saw poverty "so profound and so prevalent as to seem beyond rational remedy." Westerners in Shanghai lived in stark contrast:

> Work apart—and we did work hard—such was life for the Westerner once privileged to call himself a Shanghailander. . . . As I look back down the corridor of years, it was a time apart, a time when it seemed as though nothing had ever been different and thus never would be. In some measure, that state of mind was induced by China itself. Even though the tremors of approaching violent change were occasionally felt, it seemed that the land was too vast, the civilization, the people and their ways too ancient, for change ever to be successful. And yet, even as we lived those days, somewhere—deep below our consciousness—we sensed that this was a life that would never exist again.

In Hawaii Irene went back to work writing for the International News Service (INS). Though it was unusual for a pregnant woman to be working at a job—not to mention that her husband frowned at the idea—Irene had tallied the household budget and saw she needed to get a job. Life moved slowly in Honolulu, and she didn't find her work difficult. Then one morning she called Bert at work, and he passed on a hot tip: the Big Island of Hawaii had been hit by a monster tidal wave.

Such juicy information was too good to pass up, and Irene decided to try to scoop her husband and his competing news service, the Associated Press. Getting the news first would impress her editor on the West Coast. Heavily pregnant, she made her way to the Radio Corporation of America offices where she filed reports. She needed information from the man in charge who held a stack of telegrams coming over the wires. She decided to fake it—acting as if she were going into labor.

The sweating telegrapher, fearing that a baby would appear any minute, handed over the information she needed. Irene copied it—there were actually five tidal waves, not one—and she wrote her story. "I borrowed my terrified friend's typewriter and collated the notes under a good fast lead" and stayed until the nervous telegrapher, terrified that a baby might be coming any minute, sent the cable to INS on the mainland. That night, INS cabled back that Irene had scooped the other news services, and a $50 bonus was on its way. The extra cash, Irene cheered, "paid for the baby." Irene Leilani Kuhn arrived on March 2, 1923.

Always on the move, the Kuhns returned to Shanghai, and Bert rejoined the *China Press*. He missed the excitement of working in China. Bert lived a double life, working for the *Press* and also as an agent for the US Naval Intelligence. Irene set aside her qualms and cheerfully went along, although she worried about keeping her baby healthy.

Irene made news of her own when she became the first person to make a radio broadcast across China in 1924. She worked in a small, sheet-draped cubicle in the *Press* office, speaking into a microphone the size of a salad plate. A crank-style wall phone picked up the sound and carried it to a radio transmitting station a few miles away. A portable phonograph supplied with a dozen records completed the equipment:

> Promptly at two minutes before six that first evening I walked into the room alone, a sheaf of news dispatches from the British Reuters service in my hands. At one minute before the hour I unhooked the telephone receiver, cranked the contraption a few times, waited for a "click" at the other end. Then I said "okay," replaced the receiver quietly and tiptoed over to the mike.
>
> We broadcast by guess and by God, for while the click was supposed to be the signal that the microphone was open and I might now begin the program, I never could be sure until after the 20-minute broadcast whether I was talking to myself in a vacant room or to a small but enthusiastic audience in widely distant places.
>
> After "good evening, everyone," I played a phonograph record to give the sending station a chance to pick themselves up had anything gone awry. The musical interval also provided time for the funny homemade sets which had sprouted in Hong Kong, Soochow, Hankow, Peking, and the outports, to warm up before the "main event."

Irene took her little girl Rene to the mainland to meet the family, leaving Bert at work in Shanghai. She was in Chicago for a visit when Irene had a vision of black-clad mourners, an open grave, and a small box to be interred. Worried, she decided to rush home to Shanghai, which would take days. She was in Vancouver, Canada, with Rene, a toddler, ready to set sail, when she received a series of telegrams.

. . . husband dangerously ill best not to sail.

. . . death expected momentarily.

Bert dead.

The doctor's report stated "unknown causes," but Irene knew better and was convinced that Bert had been poisoned, something to do with his work with Naval Intelligence. She planned to stay in Chicago supporting herself and Rene by freelancing, when her old boss Phil Payne offered her a job at his new paper, the *New York Daily Mirror,* the Hearst chain's answer to the *New York Daily News.* Irene went back to covering messy divorces, high-profile murder trials, and the cross-Atlantic flight of American pilot Charles Lindbergh.

She continued to move from one job to another as she raised Rene as a widowed mother. In the early 1930s she tried a stint in Hollywood writing film scenarios for three big-name studios. But Irene missed newspaper work, forthright and factual, not the devious complications of the movie industry.

In 1933, Irene returned to New York to write features for the *World-Telegram.* She penned her memoir, *Assigned to Adventure,* sharing well-crafted stories about her days in Paris and Shanghai and profiling some big names in journalism. Irene also scooped her rivals by revealing the scandalous abdication of Great Britain's King Edward VIII, who gave up his throne to marry Mrs. Wallis Warfield Simpson, an American divorcée. She wrote about women she met and admired: First Lady Eleanor Roosevelt; actress Helen Hayes; Adele Springer, a lawyer who campaigned for safe ocean liners and who worked for world peace; and Dee Collins, the young widow of a test pilot who'd earned a living for her children as a cabaret singer in New York's Rainbow Grill.

The "tremors of approaching violent change" that Irene Kuhn had sensed during her months in Shanghai eventually shook China to pieces. Irene watched first how the early revolution of 1925 split into opposing sides as Nationalists and Communists fought to gain control of China's government. The second wave of change came from outside when, in 1931, Japan invaded and occupied Manchuria and moved south to attack Shanghai in 1932.

When the United States entered World War II in December 1941, Irene, working as a commentator with the National Broadcasting Company (NBC), found herself frozen in her job. She'd planned to leave earlier, but the US government declared broadcasting—like shipbuilding and steelmaking—an essential part of the war effort. "I couldn't leave to go back to my own writing, as I really wanted to do," she told an interviewer later, "so I turned it to advantage."

In uniform, Irene Corbally Kuhn broadcast from US Navy ships during World War II. *Irene Kuhn Papers, American Heritage Center, University of Wyoming*

The "advantage" Irene used was her experience and status as a reporter, which enabled her to score credentials as a war correspondent in the Pacific. During the war years she logged 24,277 miles in Air Corps planes in the China-Burma-India Theater. Never friendly to the idea of having women on its ships, the US Navy tolerated her presence. Irene reported from the USS *Rocky Mount*, flagship of the Pacific Fleet, when Japan surrendered to the United States. The next month, General Joseph Stillwell, commander of American forces in China, caved after repeated requests and allowed Irene into China to work.

In 1945, Irene met her goal to be the first American to broadcast from newly freed Shanghai. Every night she sat behind a microphone reporting the news, never sure that it would reach anyone. When her pleas to "please relay to San Francisco," were picked up by the Pacific Fleet, she was invited to report from the *Rocky Mount*. The ship dropped anchor at Shanghai's number-one buoy, the spot of honor traditionally reserved for a British vessel. Irene's reporter's instincts told her immediately that the United States of America was now the world's dominant nation. She, Irene Corbally Kuhn, was witness to the transformation of America into a superpower.

That September, together with another reporter and an American officer, Irene toured a former Japanese prison camp where American airmen had been imprisoned and died in 1942 and 1943, three of them executed. A Chinese colonel was in charge of the Japanese soldiers who had worked at the camp; now the Japanese were prisoners themselves.

The Chinese colonel ordered tea, and the little group sat down to be served by the Japanese. As they sipped from teacups, a small silk-wrapped box was placed on the table in front of the reporters, a delivery from the former Japanese camp commander. The box contained the ashes of a 24-year-old American flyer who had died a prisoner in his camp. In a collection of reporters' memoirs, Irene wrote, "It was a sadistic little gesture, timed to perfection, this arrival of the dead flyer's ashes in their urn inside the wooden, silk-wrapped box set down there now on top of the other box amid the teacups."

After she returned to the US, Irene Corbally Kuhn continued to broadcast for NBC and shared a program with her daughter Rene Kuhn Bryant. During these postwar days, when the Soviet Union and a rising Communist power in China led to 40 years of Cold War, Irene's conservative instincts dominated much of her writing. She took a strong stand against communism and fully believed that its zealous supporters would never stop trying to bring down Western democracy. In 1951 she wrote an article that called out the liberal-leaning *New York Times Book Review* for its pro-communist views. YOUR CHILD IS THEIR TARGET, written by Irene for the *American Legion Magazine*, warned of the dangers of American education falling to communist influences.

WOMEN DON'T BELONG IN POLITICS, said another article in 1953, Irene declaring that giving women the right to vote back into 1919 hadn't done much to change the future. As she pointed out, both women and men were voters when the United States suffered through the Great Depression and fought a world war at great cost, only to see "victory [which] we let traitors, nincompoops and ruthless political opportunists throw away as if were a soggy bun, something for the birds."

Irene Corbally Kuhn and other women reporters of her generation had lived their lives making their way in a man's world. In our eyes it seems strange that she disapproved of younger women moving into the workplace. YOU OUGHT TO GET MARRIED, read her article in the *American Mercury* in 1954. Perhaps Irene yearned for what she missed in her own life, a husband to share her achievements, sorrows, and joys. Unlike so many women writing about war, Irene never remarried after her husband's unexplained death. Throughout her life, she followed astrology and maintained a keen interest in the occult.

Well into old age, Irene kept writing. Her stories appeared in magazines as wide ranging as *American Legion*, *Good Housekeeping*, *Cosmopolitan*, and *Gourmet*. She lived to the age of 97.

Europe Between World Wars, 1919–1939

In 1919, Europeans picked up the pieces from the Great War and tried to move on. The Treaty of Versailles, signed by the Allies and Germany in 1919, thrust heavy penalties on Germany, stripped away its territories, and exacted the huge sum of $33 billion in war reparations. The Empire of Austria-Hungary was dismantled, and young republics sprang up in Poland, Czechoslovakia, Hungary, and Austria.

Under the terms of peace, Germany also established its first republic. The young democracy turned out to be a disaster, and late in the 1920s Germany lapsed into a period of massive inflation followed by a depression. Amid the joblessness, disorder, and general bitterness about paying Germany's war debts, a new political party arose seemingly from nowhere: the National Socialists, or Nazis. A fascist organization, the Nazis were backed by large numbers of German military men and industrialists who manufactured steel and armaments.

The Nazis first gained real power in 1933 when elections placed them in 44 percent of the seats in Germany's Reichstag (parliament). Their charismatic leader, Adolf Hitler, became Germany's führer ("leader"), chancellor, and commander in chief soon thereafter. With Hitler as their leader, the Nazis pledged to rescue Germany from those they hated: liberals, socialists, communists, and Jews. Hitler's government isolated German Jews by gradually stripping away their rights. Fascists also installed Benito Mussolini as Italy's dictator in 1922. In Spain the fascist General Francisco Franco, backed by German arms and air power, marshaled an army of rebels in 1936 and toppled Spain's young republican government. The Spanish Civil War was later seen as a practice run for Hitler's Germany when the Nazis invaded Poland in 1939.

All the while, the Nazis nationalized German industry, built Germany's war machine, and created the autobahn, a network of superhighways. By the end of the 1930s, Germany had annexed Austria and seized German-speaking regions of France and Czechoslovakia.

Ordinary citizens, international experts, and entire governments stayed in denial about Germany's plans to conquer Europe. Americans, caught up in the Great Depression, were content with thinking that Hitler was a problem for Britain and France to sort out. But reporters Sigrid Schultz and Dorothy Thompson sounded the call as the Nazi menace grew, though few Americans heeded their warnings. Thompson was called the "American Cassandra," an unflattering comparison to the Greek goddess who was cursed with predicting a future that no one would believe.

- -
Sigrid Schultz
- -

REPORTING FROM BERLIN

Berlin, September 1
At six AM, Sigrid Schultz—bless her heart—phoned. She said:
"It's happened." I was very sleepy—my body and mind numbed,

*paralyzed. I mumbled: "Thanks, Sigrid," and tumbled out of
bed. The war is on!*
—*William Shirer,* Berlin Diary, 1942

She was a looker. Blue-eyed and blond, fashionably dressed—
she was smart, as well—not to mention an excellent listener.
She was a gourmet cook, was said to smoke a pipe, and she gave
wonderful parties in the apartment she shared with her mother.
It seemed natural that important men from the German govern-
ment liked to drop by her desk in the *Chicago Tribune*'s bureau in
Berlin's elegant Hotel Adlon. They might have thought she was
German—she spoke like one, but she could switch to French,
Polish, Dutch, or English. And when she spoke English, her
American accent shone, because Sigrid Schultz had been born
in Chicago.

Berlin seemed an unlikely place for an American girl, but
Schultz had lived there since she was a girl. Her father, Hermann, a Norwegian painter, had been commissioned to paint
the portrait of Chicago's mayor around the time her mother,
opera singer Hedwig Jaskewitz, gave birth to Sigrid in 1893. In
1911 the family moved to Germany so her father could paint
William II, the king of Württemberg. Her father was popular
among Europe's aristocracy, so Sigrid grew up traveling the
continent and attending school in France, where she graduated
from Paris's famed Sorbonne University in 1914.

The Schultz family was in Berlin when Germany unexpectedly went to war in August 1914. But Hermann Schultz was in
poor health and couldn't leave with the other foreigners who
were allowed to leave Germany. The Schultzes were caught in
Berlin, required to check in twice daily with German police.
Hermann Schultz now found it hard to provide for his wife and
daughter. Sigrid helped out by teaching French and English to

The young Sigrid Schultz, in an Edwardian summer dress, posed with "Mommy" for a photo along a waterfront. *Wisconsin Historical Society*

well-heeled families, but she continued her own study in international law at a university.

In 1919 Sigrid's obvious flair for languages caught the eye of Richard Henry Little, who reported for the *Chicago Tribune*. She "trotted by his side, an eager cub reporter," as Little traveled through Germany gathering information firsthand for his boss, Colonel Robert R. McCormick, the *Tribune's* owner and a well-known isolationist. Little depended on Sigrid to translate for him, and the experience helped to build the self-confidence that became a trademark of her career in reporting. When Little sent her on an errand to the offices of the German navy, Sigrid was expected to walk around to a side door. Ignoring the navy rule banning women from using its main entrance, Sigrid zipped up the front steps to drop off her boss's calling card and request an interview.

Early on, the stories she heard and the events she witnessed convinced Sigrid that the uneasy peace between Germany and the Allies was a sham. In the Adlon Hotel, where Sigrid worked, lived German general Erich von Ludendorff, "whose brain conceived the nightmare now know as total war." Never mind that the Treaty of Versailles had sucked the life out of Germany's economy. Sigrid was convinced that total war was part of the German mind-set. German men and women, she warned, "take their orders from military and civilian leaders of daring and vision, with wise knowledge of human beings and the world and utter contempt for anything that does not serve their common cause—German world supremacy." Indeed, as the Allies fought their way to Germany's capital of Berlin in the waning days of World War I, Sigrid Schultz was convinced, "Germany will try it again."

Becoming Richard Little's protégé was a lucky break, because Colonel McCormick refused to allow women to sit at his Chicago city desk. However, the colonel wanted to build a solid corps of foreign correspondents, and Sigrid neatly fit his standards. By 1925, the *Tribune*'s Berlin bureau chief was sent packing to a lesser assignment in Rome, and in months, Sigrid stepped in to become America's first woman bureau chief at a foreign desk.

Sigrid had proved she could keep up with her male colleagues, especially Floyd Gibbons, the one-eyed director of the *Tribune*'s Foreign Service. She felt grateful to Gibbons, whose eye patch reminded everyone that he had been gravely injured reporting the 1918 Battle of Belleau Wood. Gibbons had no hang-ups about women's abilities as reporters; he'd already hired another young American, Irene Corbally, to work for the *Trib* in Paris. Sigrid also impressed Gibbons when he observed that she could match male reporters, drink for drink, in the Hotel Adlon bar. Sigrid didn't mention that she had quietly arranged for the bartender to leave out the alcohol.

Sigrid was gifted with instincts that led her to solid information. Quickly she picked up on what so many foreign correspondents had to learn the hard way: the art and science of "hanging around," building relationships with potential contacts and fruitful sources.

Sigrid singled out Hermann Göring, an ace pilot and rising Nazi, as a good prospect for schmoozing, and she asked him to lunch. Of all the uncouth men surrounding Hitler, Göring seemed to have the best manners. Over the years Göring and Sigrid rubbed elbows at glamorous parties that drew ambassadors, film stars, opera singers, and the Nazi elite.

This well-known photo captured Sigrid Schultz as she attended a Berlin party where she was known to US ambassador William Dodd (left) and Nazi minister of propaganda Joseph Goebbels. *Wisconsin Historical Society*

But even as she partied, Sigrid Schultz listened for the choice comment or quiet aside that made her such a good reporter. Hermann Göring eventually introduced her to Hitler himself. She was repulsed. "Hitler grabbed my hand in both of his hands and tried to look soulfully into my eyes, which made me shudder, and Hitler sensed it."

"In 1930 I realized that the Nazis would play a decisive role in European history and I began studying them most closely," she wrote. "In the first interview I had with Hitler he staggered me by asserting, at the top of his voice: 'My will shall be done,' and by showing very clearly that he felt he had the right to speak in religious terms." Why intelligent, educated men and women would accept Hitler as their leader alarmed her, when clearly the Nazis represented the worst of humanity. It seemed to her that most Germans believed Hitler's ongoing mantra that Germany lost World War I due to evil outsiders. Most but not all German women, in Sigrid's eyes, were especially mesmerized with Hitler and were quite willing to accept that Germany lost World War I due to "a treacherous betrayal of the German Army by (1) the Republic, (2) the Allies, (3) the Communists, or (4) the Jews."

Hitler, Göring, and other top Nazis kept tabs on what foreign correspondents wrote in their papers back home. When the Nazis expelled *New York Herald Tribune* writer Dorothy Thompson in 1934, they created an uproar. The Nazis had to tread carefully thereafter, but they still spied on foreign reporters. Like Thompson, Sigrid Schultz was watched by the Gestapo, Hitler's dreaded secret police. Sigrid felt sure that her maid was on the Gestapo's payroll.

The Gestapo often tried the common trick of planting information on unsuspecting journalists, "discovering" it, and putting the hapless reporters on trial for espionage. Sigrid took great care not to be tripped up by such tactics, so one day, when her mother telephoned to say that a stranger had dropped a packet of papers at her flat, Sigrid jumped up from her desk and raced home. The packet held designs for airplane engines. Sigrid threw it in the fire and watched it burn. On her way back to the Hotel Adlon, she walked past that same stranger, who now was heading to her home with two shady-looking others in tow. She boldly told the courier, a Gestapo agent, that his "evidence" was gone, hailed a cab, and ordered the driver to take her to the American embassy.

Sigrid struck back when the perfect opportunity arose at an engagement party she cohosted for Göring and his fiancée, a shy German actress. At the appropriate time, she quietly leaned over to Göring and spoke "as if exchanging chit-chat about the opera" but making her point that she despised his tactics. In return, he nicknamed her "that dragon from Chicago," an example, he said, of "people from that crime-ridden city."

The pressure kept up. In 1938, Sigrid became a radio announcer for the Mutual Broadcasting System. By the onset of World War II in September 1939, four different Nazi censors typically took their black pens to Sigrid's radio transcripts before she went on the air. Sometimes her manuscripts were so marked up she refused to broadcast at all.

Meanwhile, the mood in the United States stayed decidedly isolationistic. Just as the United States had mostly ignored the stirrings of trouble in Europe before World War I, so now Washington ignored William Dodd, the American ambassador in Berlin who warned that Germany was preparing for a second war. Sigrid's reporter's instincts led her to piece together a hideous fact: the Nazis had embarked on a program of euthanasia, so-called "mercy killings" of sick and mentally deficient children, old people, and patients with terminal diseases.

As the Nazi Party began its persecution of Jews in Germany, Sigrid watched and reported on what she observed, as bit by bit Jews were barred from schools, shops and businesses, and the opera and symphony. She took note of the concentration camps the Nazis began building in 1933 for their political prisoners. Just a few years later, the Nazis would use these camps to carry out their "final solution" of genocide as they tried to kill every Jew in Europe.

Sigrid Schultz so feared being expelled from Germany that she took a pen name, John Dickson, who filed "his" reports for the *Chicago Tribune* from "Paris." These escaped the censors, and Sigrid stayed safe working just blocks away from Nazi headquarters. She scooped every correspondent in July 1939, when her doctor, a friendly man who also had several high-level Nazis in his practice, gave her a tip: pay a visit to Hitler's astrologer, he advised, and he'll provide a lead for you to follow.

Sigrid could hardly believe her ears when the astrologer told her that Hitler was considering an alliance with the Soviet Union. After all, Hitler had preached against the Bolshevists for years. Her scoop, filed under John Dickson's byline, reported in the *Chicago Tribune* that "the newest toast in high Hitler-Guard circles is: 'To our new ally, Russia!'"

Would Germans believe their dictator? "Dickson" certainly thought so. "If Hitler says the wicked Red Soviets are no longer Red nor wicked, the Germans will accept his word!"

Sigrid was correct in her prediction. On August 24, Sigrid reported on her regular Sunday evening Mutual broadcast that Germany and the Soviet Union had signed a nonaggression pact. The agreement left Germany free to attack Poland.

On the morning of September 1, 1939, Sigrid picked up her phone to call a fellow correspondent named Bill Shirer to tell him the news: Germany had invaded Poland. She rushed to the

Reichstag to watch as Hitler made the announcement to cheering crowds. World War II had begun, no surprise at all to the dragon from Chicago. It was payback time. Sigrid knew that evil forces in Germany—a conspiracy of industry, military, and political fanatics who believed in a special destiny for the German people—had prepared for this "total war" ever since Germany had lost World War I. Her front page story—with her real name in the byline—ran later that day in the *Chicago Tribune*.

Word of German atrocities in Poland could be heard in every railroad station waiting room as black-uniformed SS men (the *Schutzstaffel*, the Nazis' elite guards) came and went on trains. A few officers complained, but they were demoted. The Nazis denied it all, saying it was propaganda from foreign countries, but at home, Sigrid recalled later, "the German people learned with surprising speed the truth about the German bestialities in Poland, as it had known about the murder of Czechs after the rape of Czechoslovakia. And why? They were told by their government—to compel them to share the guilt of what was done. On the whole the people reacted with unforgivable indifference."

Sigrid had sent her mother and her dog home to the United States in 1938, but she stayed in Germany. She took shrapnel in her leg when Britain bombed Berlin but stayed on the job until she contracted typhus during a vacation in Spain. She became so ill she couldn't return to Berlin. When the United States entered the war in December 1941, Sigrid sailed home from Portugal to live with her mother in their small cottage home in Westport, Connecticut.

Sigrid kept up her broadcasts on Mutual, and she launched a one-woman speaking tour to tell her stories about life in Hitler's Germany and her experiences with the Nazi elite. She wrote a book, *Germany Will Try It Again*, to warn Americans that, even if the Allies won the war, there would still be a strong streak of total war in the German psyche. To the surprise of many, Sigrid insisted that German women were even more fanatical than their men, how "women would fight for the privilege of touching [Hitler's] mustard-colored raincoat; some would even try to kiss its hem."

Sigrid returned to Germany in the spring of 1945. On April 10, she, Helen Kirkpatrick (also with the *Chicago Daily News*), and Marguerite Higgins of the *New York Herald Tribune* became the first women reporters to enter Buchenwald, the first concentration camp to be liberated by the Allies. Soldiers and reporters saw and smelled what the Nazis had done to human beings there. Sigrid walked through hut after hut where French prisoners—survivors—lay on wooden platforms. She used her gift for French to assure them, these living skeletons of men and boys, that the war was truly over.

Sigrid also went to Heinrich Himmler's summer retreat as reporters scoured the place looking for documents. Himmler, the notorious head of the SS, had papers stashed all over the estate. American agents had already carried off what they wanted, but boxes of papers and books were hidden in a barn. Sigrid went through boxes of documents seeking clues to Himmler's background and discovered a photo album with a woven cover and the title *Angora*. Inside were photos of angora rabbits, whose soft fur was sheared and spun into wool to line the coats of pilots, among others. Two decades later, the Wisconsin Historical Society (which houses Sigrid Schultz's papers) shared Sigrid's description of the Nazi rabbit-breeding program. Her words bore witness to the appalling evil that was the Nazi mind:

> The first picture was startling indeed; it was a huge photograph of the head of a handsome, obviously contented

angora rabbit. Other pages showed rows of hutches that were model sanitary quarters, special equipment in which the mash for the rabbits was prepared that shone as brightly as the cooking pans in a bride's kitchen. The tools used for the grooming of the rabbits could have come out of the showcases of Elizabeth Arden.

What gave special significance to the book was that under each photograph was the name of the concentration camp where it was taken. Thus, in the same compound where 800 human beings would be packed into barracks that were barely adequate for 200, the rabbits lived in luxury in their own elegant hutches. In Buchenwald, where tens of thousands of human beings were starved to death, rabbits enjoyed scientifically prepared meals. The SS men who whipped, tortured, and killed prisoners saw to it that the rabbits enjoyed loving care.

Sigrid Schultz went on to a long career in journalism. As Americans turned away from war talk in the 1950s, she turned to writing for the *Ladies' Home Journal*. Thirty years after the war ended, she told an interviewer she was appalled by ordinary Americans' poor understanding of their own history and warned that "the greatest threat to Western democracies today is our own complacency and indolence."

Sigrid herself was doing her part to record history by working on an oral history of anti-Semitism. (This is now housed in the New York Public Library.) She died in 1980, after which her little cottage in Westport, Connecticut, was torn down. Sigrid had bargained with the city to keep her home when others were knocked down for a parking lot. It had stood there for years, a small but powerful symbol of resistance by its feisty owner, that dragon from Chicago.

Dorothy Thompson

REPORTING FROM BERLIN

When I walked into Adolf Hitler's salon, I was convinced that I was meeting the future dictator of Germany. In less than 50 seconds I was sure I was not. It took just that time to measure the startling insignificance of this man who has set the world agog.
—Dorothy Thompson

When Dorothy Thompson arrived at a Berlin hotel to interview Adolph Hitler late in 1931, it crossed her mind that she should take a whiff of smelling salts to settle her nerves. Hitler was a puzzle, the leader of the Nazis, and a growing influence in Germany. His National Socialist Party was attracting a curious mix of street kids, industrialists, laborers, and office workers. But Dorothy had no cause for worry. Once in front of the Nazi leader, she sized him up as a most unimpressive person and shared her frank views in print.

He is formless, almost faceless, a man whose countenance is a caricature, a man whose framework seems cartilaginous, without bones. He is inconsequent and voluble, ill poised and insecure. He is the very prototype of the Little Man. . . . His movements are awkward. There is in his face no trace of any inner conflict or self-discipline.

And yet, he is not without a certain charm. But it is the soft, almost feminine charm of the Austrian! When he talks it is with a broad Austrian dialect. The eyes alone are notable. Dark gray and hyperthyroidic, they have the

peculiar shine which often distinguishes geniuses, alcoholics, and hysterics.

Germany had become a different country in the nine years
since Dorothy had first lived in Berlin, its capital. The Weimar
Republic was in turmoil. For a while, Germans had prospered
under their fledgling democracy. However, the staggering cost
of war reparations (payments to the victors of World War I),
followed by the Great Depression of the 1930s, had hurled Germany into hard times and burdened Germans with crushing
inflation. It was common knowledge that housewives paid for
a loaf of bread with a bushel basket full of reichsmarks, Germany's wildly inflated paper money.

As the months unfolded and Hitler rose to power, Dorothy
was harshly rebuked for underestimating him. Still, she had
good reason to question Hitler's ability to lead the *Vaterland*.
She couldn't believe that the German people, proud keepers of
their "Fatherland's" rich culture —art, books, music, religion—
would permit this lank-haired, soft-looking man to topple the
Weimar Republic and accept him as their dictator.

But in 1933 they did, and immediately Germany's new führer
and his gang of thugs shot everyone in their own party whom
they could not keep in line. This Night of the Long Knives signaled an early step in the Nazi reign of terror that endured until
April 1945, when Germany lost World War II.

In August 1934, when Dorothy was again in Berlin doing
interviews, she met a German reporter whom she respected.
Over coffee with whipped cream and fresh plum cake—a summertime favorite—he spoke approvingly of Hitler's "revolution."
"The cleanup was not pretty," he said, "but it has consolidated
Germany." The next morning, a Gestapo agent called on Dorothy in her hotel room. The young man, wearing a trench coat

like Hitler's, handed her an order to leave Germany within 48 hours. Dorothy became the first reporter expelled by the Nazis. Dorothy's impressions came out in her book, *I Saw Hitler!*, and people packed lecture halls to hear her speak. NBC liked her style and hired her as a radio commentator in 1936. Even better, the *New York Herald Tribune* gave her a plum job writing *On the Record*, running opposite top columnist Walter Lippmann. Their columns were syndicated in newspapers from coast to coast and reached millions. Dorothy's column was intended to enhance Lippmann's by targeting women, but Dorothy knew that what women read they talked about, often to their husbands. She had already married twice, and she was destined to meet husband number three.

Dorothy deserved her success, thanks to a gift for writing and the guts to go after her stories—exactly the traits reserved for hard-bitten newsmen. She was a big-boned, sturdy girl whose pink-and-white complexion contrasted sharply with her dark hair and eyes. The daughter of a Methodist minister, Dorothy lost her mother when she was seven and had a disastrous relationship with her stepmother. At 14, Dorothy was sent from home in Hamburg, New York, to live with her father's sisters in Chicago. There, free of her stepmother's Victorian restrictions, she blossomed.

Dorothy Thompson was hard to miss, and it was in her nature to shine. She rollerskated to class at the top-notch Lewis Institute, a type of junior college in Chicago, where she joined a group of boys on the debate team, and she burst onto campus at Syracuse University in 1912 with status as a junior. She soaked up all that a classical liberal arts curriculum had to offer: mathematics, sciences, foreign language, history, and literature. She graduated with that dream shared by so many students in love with learning: Dorothy wanted to be a writer. But she had a younger sister and brother, and it was understood that Dorothy would help to pay for their college expenses.

She settled for a job with a women's suffrage group in western New York and then moved into social work, which left her dissatisfied and ready to leave the country with her friend Barbara de Porte in 1919. Dorothy was 27, equipped with a hazy notion that she'd get herself to Russia to see its revolution for herself.

Dorothy set sail for London with a plan to land freelance work—the best way for a girl reporter to get herself hitched to a daily newspaper. Aboard ship she saw her first opportunity to get a good story when she met a group of Zionists, Jews who sought to establish a Jewish nation in the Holy Land. She asked them questions, and she listened carefully; and once on land, she submitted an article to the INS, which was accepted. To pay her bills, she wrote publicity at a penny per page for the American Red Cross, all the while tracking interesting stories to build her credibility as a journalist.

Dorothy gathered her share of rejections when she first submitted articles to news services, but her straight talk and self-assured manner served her well. She interviewed an Irish revolutionary, Terence MacSwiney, a reputed leader of the rebel Sinn Fein party. It turned out to be his final interview; MacSwiney was imprisoned by the British and died of starvation after he went on a hunger strike to protest British rule over Ireland. The INS sent her to Rome to write about a general workmen's strike, an early warning of the rise of Benito Mussolini and his Fascist followers.

With each freelance piece, Dorothy inched closer toward her goal. In the fall of 1920, with regular work for the INS and Red Cross, she felt confident enough to move to Paris, one of hundreds of young Americans attracted to the City of Light.

She stayed just a few months, and then, on a tip from a *Chicago Daily News* editor, she moved to Vienna, Austria, for a better look at central Europe's troubles. Young, untested republics in Germany and Austria faced uncertain futures.

The Philadelphia *Public Ledger* offered Dorothy credentials to use in Vienna and agreed to receive articles on spec and pay for those that it published. That understanding was better than no agreement at all, and Dorothy enhanced it by finding herself a mentor named Marcel Fodor, an Austrian newsman who worked for Britain's *Manchester Guardian*. They worked as a pair, spending so much time together that others assumed they were lovers. For Dorothy, however, this relationship was strictly one of work and friendship, and it worked well.

In October 1921, Dorothy struck journalistic gold when she tracked a rumor that loyalists planned to return Hungary's former Emperor, Charles IV, back to his throne. The ex-emperor and his wife were held in a castle outside Budapest, forbidden to speak with the outside world. Thompson wrote for the Red Cross in Budapest and used her connections to her advantage. She donned the outfit of a Red Cross nurse and talked her boss into masquerading as a doctor. They made their way into the castle and spoke at length with Charles and his devoted wife, Zita von Bourbon-Parma. The anxious empress wrote a note to their son telling him they were safe, and Dorothy smuggled it out. Dorothy's scoop beat every other newspaper, and the grateful *Public Ledger* gave her a steady job soon thereafter.

Now Dorothy was on the move, a mark of her career as she jumped jobs, seizing each opportunity like a mountain lion in the fur coat she wore. In Vienna she fell in love with the German language and its unique Austro-German culture. She befriended artists, intellectuals, government officials, and ordinary Austrians. She drank *capuchiner* in Vienna's celebrated cafés, enjoyed concerts and plays, and wore long dresses to elegant dinners, all the while keeping an eye on any stories she could develop.

Dorothy kept pace with her male colleagues, who were in friendly competition with her, and though a scoop was to be admired, they often shared sources and backed each other when necessary. In 1925, when word arrived on one such evening that war was brewing in Poland, she was said to leave in her gown and party slippers directly for Warsaw. She disappeared another time, and when a carload of reporters was attacked by gunfire, *Chicago Tribune* reporter Floyd Gibbons assumed she was dead and filed an obituary, only for Dorothy to show up alive and well. The newspapermen who worked alongside her admired how she worked very, very hard.

Dorothy surrounded herself with people, treasured her friendships, and relished being the center of attention. Everywhere she worked she could count on friends for backup and sophisticated conversation. She became friends with Rose Wilder Lane, a Missouri girl with a zest for life who shared a gift for storytelling with her mother, Laura Ingalls Wilder. The letters that flew back and forth between Dorothy and Rose went on to fill a book long after they were dead.

Dorothy felt passionate about her women friends and possibly became lovers with several. However, she liked men equally well and expected marriage to give her both a permanent residence and someone to be the rock in her topsy-turvy life. In 1922, she fell head over heels for Josef Bard, an aspiring Austrian intellectual who turned out to be a dandy with a wandering eye. Between Bard's philandering and Thompson's hectic lifestyle, it was clear that they'd made a mistake, and they divorced five years later.

Thompson wasn't single for long. She threw herself a 34th birthday party, and a friend brought a guest, America's leading

novelist Sinclair Lewis. A Midwesterner like Dorothy, the spare
and acne-scarred Lewis had written *Main Street*, a smash hit
novel that slammed life in small-town America. Lewis, nicknamed "Red" for his hair, proposed marriage the night they
met, and Thompson telephoned her downstairs neighbor the
next morning to ask if she should accept.

In days they became engaged, despite the neighbor's candid
warning that Red (whose family called him "Hal") Lewis was
a drunk. The gifted Lewis was a complicated man, delightful
when he chose to be and a skunk when he didn't, as Thompson
well knew. Still, as she wrote to Rose Lane, at the mature age of
34 she had a new view on love and on loving Hal Lewis:

> I approach life with more humor. . . . I am not nearly
> so much "in love"—whatever that may mean. I cannot
> stretch my imagination to believe that SL is the most beau-
> tiful person in the world. I know him to be compounded
> of bad habits, weaknesses, irritabilities, irritancies. But
> . . . he amuses me: the first requirement of a husband.
> He heightens my sense of life. He opens a future for me,
> so that for the first time in years, I dream of tomorrow,
> as well as enjoy today. Thus, he gives me back a gift of
> youth.

Dorothy and Hal set up housekeeping on a Vermont farm
with two homes. Thompson claimed to be delighted when baby
Michael was born in 1930, and she also acted as stepmother to
Wells Lewis, Hal's son from his first marriage. But in Thompson's imperial view of life, giving birth was one thing, and caring for a newborn baby quite another. She had work to do, not
to mention that a squalling child would annoy Hal. The solution, she decided, was to lodge Michael and his trained nurse

Dorothy Thompson, nicknamed "The Blue-Eyed Tornado" and "The American Cassandra," was a household name in the late 1930s. *Dorothy Thompson Collection, Special Collections Center, Syracuse University Library*

in another house on their farm. That winter, the family lived in New York, and Thompson left for a "fast trip" to Germany and Russia, which to her meant two months on the road. Rose Lane came to run the household.

For Michael Lewis, life with "Mother" was always a series of fast trips for her and long months for him moving from one boarding school to the next. For many boys in well-off families, childhood was like that: a series of boarding schools and summer camps, broken up by family holidays with nursemaids and nannies in tow. Sometimes these boys achieved real intimacy with their parents, but many like Michael seemed more like symbols of children than real kids with scraped knees, chicken pox, and homework. Michael, though bright enough, didn't share his parents' gifts for intense study and showed a lack of trying that puzzled his mother. He never seemed to fit in. Michael never achieved his goal to be a respected actor; he had inherited his father's affection for alcohol and was hard to work and live with.

Michael Lewis was barely walking when his mother interviewed Adolph Hitler in 1931. Three years later she returned to Berlin. As she wrote for *Harper's* magazine, Germany was a different country than the one she'd left in 1931. When she motored from Austria into Bavaria, she spotted flags hanging from all the houses—bright red with a white circle bearing a black swastika in the middle. Election banners spanned the streets, but they touted only one candidate: Adolph Hitler.

Dorothy stopped in Garmisch and chatted up a tourist from Chicago. He had been at the Passion Play in Oberammergau and had harsh words for the Germans in the audience. "'These people are all crazy,' he said. 'This is not a revolution; it's a revival. They think Hitler is God. Believe it or not, a German woman sat next to me at the Passion Play, and when they hoisted Jesus on the cross, she said, 'There he is. That is our Fuehrer, Our Hitler.'"

German kids were assembled into the Nazi machine as well. Dorothy drove past a large camp for Hitler Youth, which could have looked like any Boy Scout camp but for an enormous banner that stretched across a hillside. It was so huge that 6,000 campers could see it from anywhere. "It was white," she told her *Harper's* readers, "and there was a swastika painted on it, and beside the only seven words, seven immense black words: WE WERE BORN TO DIE FOR GERMANY!"

Dorothy had been back in Germany only 10 days when the Nazi government expelled her. The expulsion hit American newspapers with a giant splash. DOROTHY THOMPSON EXPELLED BY REICH FOR 'SLUR' ON HITLER, roared the *New York Times* on August 26.

If anything, Hitler's act made Dorothy even more of a celebrity among Americans. In 1936, the *New York Herald Tribune* asked her to write a thrice-weekly column to explain the political climate to women readers. Syndicated to 150 newspapers, Dorothy became a household name, writing about everything that crossed her mind. Her second job working as a commentator for NBC Radio also helped propel her to popularity. In 1939, *Time* magazine named her the second most popular woman in

In 1939 Dorothy Thompson told a Senate committee that the United States had no business remaining neutral in the face of a menacing Nazi Germany. *Library of Congress LC-DIG-hec-26561*

the United States. The top spot was owned by First Lady Eleanor Roosevelt.

Dorothy Thompson became known as "the American Cassandra." Like the cursed Greek princess who could see into the future, she predicted that Adolph Hitler would bring the world to war. As in Cassandra's tale, few listened to what Dorothy had to say. Not until 1941, when Japan destroyed the Pacific Fleet at Pearl Harbor, Hawaii, did the United States join the Allies to battle both Japan and Hitler's Germany in World War II.

Dorothy continued to rail against Hitler as Germany carried out its program of isolating its Jewish citizens. She began a campaign to expose the plight of Jewish refugees trying to flee Europe, people turned away by immigration laws in Britain and the United States. She captured the attention of President Franklin D. Roosevelt, who seemed to heed her warnings about the dangers of Nazi Germany, and she became his advisor. Her support of a Democrat in the White House infuriated her publishers, Helen Rogers Reid and her son Ogden, owners of the *New York Herald Tribune,* both steadfast conservatives and isolationists. The Reids did not renew Dorothy's contract, and she moved on.

Dorothy Thompson and Sinclair Lewis divorced in 1940. Her career had risen ever brighter; his star among American authors had fallen long before. Dorothy met her third and final husband, the Czech artist Maxim Kopf, when he came to paint her portrait. Kopf was on his third marriage, one more of convenience than love, and it took Dorothy $30,000 to convince his wife to set Maxim free to marry her. In 1943, Dorothy got her wish and embarked on the happiest years of her life. Maxim sensed that Dorothy needed security and a steady hand so as to keep up her nonstop public persona. After all, she was known as "the Blue-Eyed Tornado."

As happy as her new husband made her, Dorothy's stellar career started a slow trek downhill after World War II. She had been a strong supporter of Zionism long ago on her first sailing to Europe, but now the movement for a Jewish homeland distressed her. As Great Britain made plans to carve out the nation of Israel from its territory in the Holy Land, it left open the question of where one million Palestinian Arabs would live. Their abandonment went against Dorothy's strong sense of fair play.

When the United Nations recognized the state of Israel in 1948, Dorothy feared that Israel would become a members-only club. In her book *On the Record*, she criticized the UN for ignoring "the opposition of the whole Arab and Moslem world," and grew even more strident as she traveled to Arab capitals, seeking the truth about their people and cultures. She fought the trend in American politics and journalism to avoid any criticism of Israel's policy toward its Arab population.

Although Dorothy's editors warned her to stay quiet, she lashed out at the Israeli government for neglecting the Palestinians who lost their homes in the new Jewish state. Such criticism of Israel was largely professional suicide in the years following World War II, and Dorothy was tagged as an anti-Semite, a smear she hotly disputed. She struggled for her right to voice her opinion, unpopular as it was, but she won little support.

As her national reputation took a plunge, Dorothy Thompson's marriage seemed to spark a change that set her in a new direction. She started writing for *McCall's*, a well-established woman's magazine, and she began to take stock of her long life. She collected a series of essays she had written for *McCall's* and published them in 1957 as *The Courage to Be*.

Dorothy wrote a lovely tribute to "Red" Lewis in 1960, even as she procrastinated for years in writing her own autobiography. She insisted she wanted to cement her place in the history of American writers, but in the end, Dorothy Thompson, who had so much to say about the world around her, left no words for herself. In early January 1961, on a visit to Portugal to see her cherished grandsons, she had a heart attack and was hospitalized. She died a few weeks later, alone in her hotel room.

3

A Second World War
1939–1945

Hungry for natural resources to feed its steel mills and factories, Japan launched its conquest of Asia in 1931. Especially tempting was China's Manchuria province, due west of Japan, and its dependency Korea, an underpopulated region rich in coal, minerals, and empty farmland. Japan began its encroachment of Manchuria in 1931, renaming it Japanese "Manchukuo." In 1932, Japan's military moved south and attacked Shanghai, China's key port.

The "tremors of approaching violent change" that Irene Kuhn had sensed in Shanghai became real in 1937 as Japan's army swept south through China into Nanking, Han-k'ou (Hankow), and Canton. Japan was a parliamentary democracy in name only; its weak government at home could not contain its powerful, aggressive generals. By 1937, the Japanese also forced their

way northward into Inner Mongolia and China's northern prov-
inces. Japan's government fell under the growing power of its
military, and by 1941 Japanese General Tōjō Hideki ruled Japan,
its parliament abolished and its emperor only a figurehead.

On December 7, the Japanese navy attacked an unsuspecting
US Pacific Fleet at Pearl Harbor, Hawaii. The next day, President
Franklin D. Roosevelt asked the US Congress to declare war
on Japan. Germany and Italy then declared war on the United
States, and the United States responded with its declaration on
December 11, 1941.

Martha Gellhorn

REPORTING FROM MADRID,
CHUNGKING, AND NORMANDY

*I think the world is just as awful as it can be at any given
moment, and then a second number of people appear at any
given moment and try to keep it from being unbearably awful.*

—Martha Gellhorn

When she was a young journalist getting her start, Janine di
Giovanni interviewed and wrote about Martha Gellhorn,
America's best-known woman war correspondent. Gellhorn,
nearly six decades older than di Giovanni, was idolized by young
women who were getting their start as journalists. During
that interview, Martha Gellhorn stated firmly that di Giovanni
was not to mention Gellhorn's marriage to the Nobel Prize–
winning novelist Ernest Hemingway.

Di Giovanni's book agent disagreed, telling her that the Hemingway information was necessary to her piece on Gellhorn, so di Giovanni included him. When Gellhorn read the piece, she was furious. Martha Gellhorn had good reason for her bitterness; Hemingway had cheated on her, both personally and professionally.

The daughter of a German-American doctor and his reform-minded wife, Martha Gellhorn grew up in St. Louis, Missouri. Edna Gellhorn campaigned for women's suffrage and took Martha with her to suffrage events. Her father was equally open-minded about women's roles in life, and Martha grew up understanding that she was to make a difference in the world. She went east to college at Bryn Mawr, one of the selective Seven Sisters women's colleges, but she lasted three years and left, ready to get a job. She never looked back.

It was April 1930. At 20, Martha Gellhorn knew what she wanted. She worked as a cub reporter for a time at the Albany, New York, *Times Union*, and then her parents fronted her enough cash to start life in Paris, which was still the beacon for young Americans on the move in the early 1930s. She paid for her berth by writing travel material for the Holland America cruise line and arrived in France with $75, two suitcases, and a typewriter. She did odd jobs and wrote what she could, selling stories to various magazines and newspapers. She took a lover, the Frenchman Bertrand de Jouvenel, heir to a family of French literary figures and a married man. Juvenal had a reputation. His father's second wife, the popular author Colette, had seduced him at age 16.

Martha and Bertrand traveled in France and Germany, and what Martha saw of Germany's Nazis disgusted her. Bertrand got a divorce and wanted Martha to marry him, but she balked at the idea of living with and rearing his small son. In 1931 she returned to the United States to look for a publisher for her first book, later to dismiss it as the forgettable effort of a raw beginner. All her life, it would frustrate Martha that she was far better at writing nonfiction, though she went on to write many more novels and short stories, always striving to write something better.

Like many gifted young adults during the Depression, Martha took a job with the Federal Emergency Relief Administration (FERA). Harry Hopkins, Franklin D. Roosevelt's trusted overseer of the FERA, handpicked Martha and 15 others to travel across the country to interview America's poor and file reports on what they saw. Martha, the youngest of the group, was dispatched to the textile mill towns of New England and the South whose malnourished poor lived in squalor. Martha's limited wardrobe, a Schiaparelli designer suit she'd bought in Europe, contrasted sharply with the rags others wore; in one home, father and son had to share a pair of good pants and shoes. The poverty and complete lack of dignity among the people she interviewed outraged her.

In due course, Martha went west to work and caused a riot in Coeur d'Alene, Idaho. Thinking that publicity would shed light on the poverty in town, she urged some down-and-out working men to break windows at the FERA office. The US government, of course, couldn't have one of its own behaving like an anarchist, and Hopkins fired her.

Martha had held onto the notes she had made as she wrote up her findings for Washington, and she used them to write a book, *The Trouble I've Seen*, published in 1936. Its four novellas, rooted in her experiences on the road, follow the lives of five people, young and old, caught in the desperation of poverty— Mrs. Maddison for one, dressing up to go to the welfare office, and 11-year-old Ruby, turning tricks for grown men "so that she can buy herself candy and a pair of roller skates." Martha was angry that people had to live that way, and her fury drove her development as a writer. Some people wrote for money, some for fame, and some to create magical worlds or to work out deep psychological problems. Martha Gellhorn wrote because she was mad about social injustice.

That December Martha, her mother, and her brother vacationed in the Florida Keys. They stopped at a bar for drinks one afternoon, and in walked Ernest Hemingway, author of two sensational books. Never one to shy away from a pretty girl—Martha's blond hair and long legs certainly qualified her—Ernest chatted her up. The charming Ernest, whose wife and dinner guests were waiting at home, was charmed by Martha as well. Not only was she a looker, she had interesting things to say. Ernest missed dinner.

Ernest Hemingway left for Spain that fall to report on the Spanish Civil War. The young Republic of Spain, championed by a mix of urban and rural workers and educated middle-class people, faced a revolt by Fascist rebels backed by Spain's big landowners, its military, and elements of the Catholic Church. The war-loving Ernest couldn't resist the lure of writing about the gallant defenders of the Spanish Republic, even if naysayers said the republicans were communist sympathizers. Off he went, with plans to report on the Spanish war for the North American News Agency and to make a film about it too.

Martha armed herself with a letter from *Collier's*, a national magazine, which promised that if she found a good war story and wrote it well, *Collier's* would buy it. For Martha Gellhorn, "Marty" to her family and friends, that letter of introduction was all she needed. She boarded a ship and sailed to Europe in search of war stories—and Ernest Hemingway. Ernest, on the skids with his wife, took Marty both as his literary protégé and his lover.

However, when it came to writing, Martha Gellhorn was a natural. *The Trouble I've Seen* had been well received, and when Martha sent her first story, "High Explosive for Everyone," to *Collier's*, editors changed the title and published it immediately. Martha was on hand in Madrid, living in a hotel, when the armies of rebel commander General Francisco Franco, backed by bombers supplied by Nazi Germany, bombarded Spain's capital. Her words, clear and direct, pulled readers into the hours of quiet fear as Madrid's beleaguered people tried to live normally between attacks. One moment, she observed, a group of housewives could be standing in line for food, the next, running for their lives:

> After all, they have been waiting there for three hours and the children expect food at home. In the Plaza Major, the shoeblacks stand around the edges of the square, with their little boxes of creams and brushes, and passers-by stop and have their shoes polished as they read a paper or gossip together. When the shells fall too heavily, the shoeblacks pick up their boxes and retreat a little way into a side street.
>
> Then for a moment it stops. An old woman, with a shawl over her shoulders, holding a terrified thin little boy by the hand, runs out into the square. You know what she is thinking: she is thinking she must get the child home, you are always safer in your own place, with the things you know. Somehow you do not believe you can get killed when you are sitting in your own parlor, you never think that. She is in the middle of the square when the next one comes.
>
> A small piece of twisted steel, hot and very sharp, sprays off from the shell; it takes the little boy in the throat. The old woman stands there, holding the hand of

the dead child, looking at him stupidly, not saying anything, and men run out toward her to carry the child. At
their left, at the side of the square, is a huge, brilliant sign
which says: GET OUT OF MADRID.

Twenty-first century readers are comfortable with first person, present tense. But Martha's writing reflected new trends in
the 1920s and '30s. Gone were the flowery sentences favored by
Victorians. During World War I, Bessie Beatty's and Louise Bryant's articles showed remnants of Victorian style, but Martha's
straightforward prose fit with writers of her generation, among
them Ernest Hemingway, John dos Passos, Dorothy Parker, and
F. Scott Fitzgerald, who wrote in a terse, realistic style.

Martha was tough and outdoorsy, easily keeping up with
Hemingway as he mingled at the front with American volunteers, the Abraham Lincoln Brigade, fighting for the Spanish
Republic. She wrote about them too, these good-natured kids
who had morphed into a fine group of soldiers.

Martha and Ernest traced the path of that summer's offensive
at Brunete, Spain, riding in a camouflaged army staff car and
a Ford roadster trailing a tattered American flag. They drove
across an open plain, stopping first at the town of Villanueva de
la Cañada. Just as they entered the bombed-out village, rebels
shelled them from the hills above the plain. As she took cover,
Martha marveled how small purple flowers had sprung up from
ground burned dark by firebombs. She went to an American
hospital where she met more volunteers, a young American
nurse whose husband was fighting, and a badly injured soldier
who apparently had created a job for himself:

The boy was shy, with young brown cheeks and brown
eyes and a crew haircut. He said he was the hospital

publicity agent and would be delighted to show me around or tell me anything I wanted to know. He said, on the other hand, it was a new job, and he didn't actually know much about it. It came out slowly that he was a graduate student at Harvard and had been in Spain since last spring. He had come in time for Brunete. It seemed he was now the hospital publicity agent because he couldn't walk very fast. He didn't want to go home, and he had been "a guest in this hospital" for a long time (and he said it with such style, such modesty), so they gave him a job.

What happened was that he was on the road to Brunete, with seven men from his company, when a bomber and some pursuit planes flew over, and that was the story. He had 38 stitches across his stomach where a fragment of a bomb had torn it open. He said they just lay there and watched the bombers coming over, and heard the pursuit planes dive on them and there was nothing much to do except lie there and pray. He told it as plainly as that, when at last he talked.

Martha's war coverage shaped both her worldview and her writing. She cared little for politics, diplomacy, military strategy, or the stuff of presidents, kings, and dictators. She had a full-blown hatred of governments. What moved her was the plight of ordinary folks whom she met, regular soldiers at the front, and innocent civilians whose lives were turned upside down by war. Liberal though she was in her politics, Martha Gellhorn despised the Communist totalitarians of the Soviet Union and Communist China as much as the Fascists, Nazis, and overzealous nationalists on the far right.

Martha Gellhorn and Ernest Hemingway were together for five years when Ernest got a divorce from his second wife.

They were married by a justice of the peace in a railroad office in Wyoming on November 21, 1940, and ate moose for dinner. Soon thereafter, *Collier's* asked Martha for a series of articles on Asia, where Japan and China had fought a war since the early 1930s. Martha's *Collier's* editor assumed it was a matter of time until Japan "would soon start destroying the East as its Axis partners Germany and Italy were destroying the West."

At the time the United States held an official policy of neutrality, but Martha believed that Americans would be sucked into the war and that the world she knew would change forever. "Hurry, hurry, before it's too late," she said to herself. She wanted to see the China she had read about in books.

Martha dragged her new husband along, though Ernest would have preferred to stay put in Cuba. He was taking life easy after long months of hard writing and looking forward to the publication of *For Whom the Bell Tolls*, his classic tale about the Spanish Civil War. (His dedication said, "This book is for Martha Gellhorn.")

The first leg of their journey, by ship from the West Coast to Hawaii, was a rough crossing of sliding furniture, crashing meal trays, and spilled liquor bottles, topped off by a traditional aloha welcome with piles of leis and a swarm of paparazzi. Hemingway, who detested such puffery, had "a face of black hate," and Martha nicknamed her husband U.C.—Unwilling Companion—in letters home.

Matters improved when they boarded a Pan Am clipper for Hong Kong—the elegant flying boat followed an island-hopping route across the South Pacific, splashing down in harbors each night to refuel and provide a hotel bed for its well-dressed passengers. When they arrived in the British colony of Hong Kong, from where they'd stage their travels into China, Martha made plans to fly inland to Lashio, at the start of the Burma Road, the

700-mile trail that wound north to Kunming, China. With the Japanese army in Manchuria to the north and the surrounding Hong Kong in the south, could the Burma Road survive as the sole supply line into China?

As Martha did her reporter's work getting the feel of exotic Hong Kong, Hemingway set up shop in their hotel bar, gathering a fan club of reporters, diplomats, businessmen, and crooks. They swapped stories as they shared in long bouts of drinking, and Hemingway adored it. He sent Martha off on her own, kindly enough, she supposed, with the comment that "M. is going off to take the pulse of the nation."

Martha's forays into China took her across vast amounts of territory, but there was little actual action for her to cover. One of her best pieces from her trip was her first: an article about her flight from Hong Kong inland to the Burma Road with China National Aviation Corporation (CNAC), whose two DC-3s and three DC-2s were both uncomfortable and dangerous. The five "small tatty planes" captained by American pilots, sometimes had a copilot on board, sometimes not.

Four days after her arrival in Hong Kong, Martha left for Lashio. She took off at 4:30 AM on a CNAC DC-2, with seven other passengers and a lone crewman, pilot Roy Leonard. "The passengers," she wrote, "were given a rough brown blanket and a brown paper bag for throwing up." The airplane climbed out of the harbor basin that was Hong Kong and over the mountains into Japanese-controlled territory. In effect, the CNAC flight was a second Burma Road into free China, a lifeline carrying $55 million in wads of Chinese currency and 5,000 kilos of mail inland and returning with tin and wolfram, a mineral used in steelmaking.

Their first stop, Chungking (now spelled Chonqing), sat on a cliff overlooking the Yangtze River, where Leonard landed on an island airstrip. They flew on to Kunming, Leonard dipping and bobbing to make sure the air was clear of Japanese planes. Their last leg took them into Lashio after 10 PM that night. Roy Leonard had flown for 16 hours—nearly 1,500 miles—a weekly routine for him. He amazed Martha, whose legs were stiff with cold and whose brain felt befuddled and oxygen deprived.

Up early the next morning, Martha wandered through a village bazaar, waiting to start the flight home after the Japanese daily air raid over Kunming, its first stop. Radio reports said the Japanese were late in bombing Kunming that day, so the CNAC flight was delayed. When they landed in Kunming at 5:30 PM the bombing had left "a city shrouded in smoke and lit by fires."

Martha had seen war in Spain, Czechoslovakia, and Finland, but nothing looked as blown away as Kunming, destruction "in a class by itself." But even as the Japanese tried to bomb away the city every day, its residents repaired the damage. They worked silently, even small kids, no sound but hammers as people tried to fix their bombed-out homes. "Endurance," Martha learned, "was the Chinese secret weapon. The Japanese should have understood that, and everybody else had better remember it."

Martha liked to hang out with the CNAC pilots and their wives, finding them much more to her taste than either Ernest's crowd of admirers or the stuffy Western expatriates who lived large in Hong Kong. As soon as she moved beyond the Western enclave along the Hong Kong harbor and into Chinese neighborhoods, she began to see how desperate and degraded the lives of everyday Chinese were. She wandered the stinking streets of the Chinese quarter, with its brothels, gambling parlors, firecrackers, sleeping cubicles, and drug dens. There, for a few cents, a "coolie" could buy a pipeful of opium pills that cost less than food, cut the appetite, and relaxed skinny, starving men who labored 12 hours per day.

This was the worst poverty Martha had ever witnessed, and she was horrified. Everywhere she went in China, she encountered the same. Martha couldn't forget the pavement sleepers in cities, bent-over peasants in the countryside, lepers with missing noses, people hawking and spitting everywhere, and everyone stinking of sweat and "night soil."

She and Ernest made their trips into free China escorted by a translator, Mr. Ma, who had a bright smile and a dim command of English. They rode by car and truck, up and down rivers by motorboat and sampan, overland by uncommonly small horses, and sometimes on foot. It poured rain in that cold spring of 1941, and Martha's writings spoke of mud, fleas, bedbugs, sewage, Mr. Ma's smiling but useless interpretations, and Ernest's miniature horse that slipped, only to have Ernest pick it up and carry

Martha Gellhorn posed with her then-husband Ernest Hemingway as she wrote about the Sino-Japanese war for *Collier's* magazine. *Ernest Hemingway Collection. John F. Kennedy Presidential Library and Museum, Boston.*

it. Martha was miserable, and several times her new husband reminded her that coming to China was her idea.

They never saw any fighting—the Nationalist Chinese army operated as a defensive force but didn't directly attack the Japanese occupiers. Yet they admired the Chinese soldiers they met, who earned even less than the pitiful coolies, and marveled at their endurance. Soldiers often went barefoot and lived for years isolated in the countryside far from home. There was no mail service to bring news of their families, a point that did not matter, Martha related wryly, because the soldiers couldn't read. Ernest stood in the rain to make rousing speeches to the forgotten men, whom he admired for their toughness and skill. Ernest, who had watched them stage a mock assault, had an eye for that kind of thing and knew these troops were well trained.

Ernest flattered the generals they met and engaged them in long sessions of drinking each other under the table, a show of hospitality among the Nationalist officers. Martha noticed that the generals lived in relative comfort in cities far from the camps in far-flung places where their soldiers lived and trained.

Martha and Ernest traveled into Chungking, free China's capital, courtesy of the Nationalists. They were caught off guard when a Dutch woman asked if they'd like to meet Chou En-lai, a name that meant nothing to Martha. She and Ernest gave their government escort the slip and were taken, at times blindfolded, to the man who was second-in-command to Communist leader Mao Tse-tung (Mao Zedong). Educated in France and equipped with an urbane air, Chou, though he used a translator, obviously understood the conversation. Martha liked him immediately. She felt at home with him, the first and only time she had that rapport with someone in China. But she couldn't write about Chou in an American magazine like *Collier's*—China's politics were far too touchy, and Martha felt constrained by the fact that she and Ernest were guests of the Nationalist government.

Quite the opposite was her introduction to Nationalist China's power couple, Chiang Kai-shek and his elegant wife Soong May-ling. Chiang had married well: Madame Chiang's father was Charlie Soong, a rich and powerful businessman who had an American education. Madame Chiang, educated at Wellesley College in Massachusetts, spoke excellent English and behaved like a co-ruler. Madame shared Chiang's utter hatred of both the Japanese, who had invaded her country, and the Chinese Communists, who threatened the Nationalists from inside. The couple kept close diplomatic ties to Washington, and most Americans viewed them as the saviors of democracy in China against the Communists.

Madame Chiang and Ernest were having a pleasant chat when Martha interrupted. Why, she asked, did China force its lepers to beg in the streets? Madame Chiang went ballistic. She retorted that the Chinese "were humane and civilized, unlike Westerners; they would never lock lepers away out of contact with other mortals." She lectured Martha with words that bit: "China had a great culture when your ancestors were living in trees and painting themselves blue."

Clearly, Chiang and his wife had no concern for the well-being of China's millions of people. This was no democracy; any notion of a free China was a joke. Again Martha felt that she couldn't share her opinions publicly. It would be bad manners, not to mention grossly undiplomatic, to criticize Chiang and his wife in print. It was a tough lesson for Martha Gellhorn, who felt she had compromised her integrity as a journalist.

In the end, Martha's journey to China, for which she'd had such high hopes, left her exhausted and deflated. Ernest had far more fun, and he criticized her gloom. "He saw the Chinese as people, while I saw them as a mass of downtrodden, valiant, doomed humanity. Long ago . . . U.C. declared as dogma 'M. loves humanity but can't stand people,'" said Martha later, quoting Ernest. "The truth was that in China I could hardly stand anything."

They took up married life in Ernest's villa in Cuba, but when the United States entered World War II that December, Martha left for Europe. Her long absences—this one for months—irked her husband, but she was not content to be simply Mrs. Ernest Hemingway. She urged Ernest to join her in England and proposed that he write for *Collier's*.

Ernest stayed in Cuba as Martha kept writing. *Collier's* paid well, and she generated 26 articles between 1938 and early 1944. Ernest's mood worsened, and their marriage began to crack. When Martha finally returned home, their relationship turned into all-out war. Ernest changed his mind about going back to journalism and secured credentials as a war correspondent—for *Collier's*.

As a big-name author, Ernest overshadowed Martha's credentials. He would be higher paid, and worse, Ernest was now the *Collier's* reporter with a guaranteed seat on a seaplane to Europe. D-Day was coming, and both Ernest and Martha planned to cover the coming Allied assault on the beaches of France. Ernest had official credentials, and Martha didn't. Ernest Hemingway had upstaged Martha at *Collier's*, when any magazine would have welcomed him to write its cover story.

While Ernest few comfortably in an airplane, Martha made her way to Europe on a Norwegian freighter loaded with amphibious assault boats and dynamite. When she arrived at London's Dorchester Hotel, she found Ernest spending time with a lively blond reporter named Mary Welsh, who worked at the London bureau for *Time*, *Life*, and *Fortune* magazines.

When word reached London that D-Day had begun, Martha wandered the docks looking for some way to get across the English Channel to Normandy. She managed to stow away on a hospital ship, hoping to be taken for a nurse if anyone spotted her. Martha went ashore at Omaha Beach and trailed stretcher bearers recovering wounded soldiers, Americans and Germans alike. She was discovered when she went back to England, and the military banished her to a training camp for American nurses. Still, she got some satisfaction knowing that Ernest had to settle for observing D-Day from a landing craft; his feet never touched the ground in France. Their invasion stories ran in *Collier's* that summer; critics would observe later that Martha wrote the better piece. She worked steadily for *Collier's* throughout the war; Ernest also did war reporting and courted Mary Welsh.

Martha and Ernest divorced in 1946. For the rest of her life, Martha Gellhorn had little good to say about Ernest Hemingway.

After the war, maternal instincts stirred, and Martha went to Italy to adopt a little boy whom she nicknamed Sandy. The slim, chain-smoking Martha kept her weight at 125 pounds no matter what, and Sandy was a pudgy child. Martha equated obesity with laziness and never forgave Sandy for being fat. He proved to be a huge disappointment to her, and in her blunt style, she told him so. When she married again in 1963 to a *Time* editor named Tom Matthews (they divorced nine years later), she got on far better with her stepson, also named Sandy.

Martha Gellhorn became the 20th century's most famous woman war correspondent. Her best-recognized piece arose out of her visit to the Nazi death camp at Dachau in April 1945. A few days behind Marguerite Higgins and Margaret Bourke-White, Martha arrived as railroad cars had been cleared and their dead human cargo buried. But the horror lingered. "Behind the barbed wire and the electric fence," she wrote for *Collier's*, "the skeletons sat in the sun and searched themselves for lice. They have no age and no faces; they all look alike and like nothing you will ever see if you are lucky." Ernest Hemingway could not have penned words any more devastating.

Martha went on to report from war zones around the world, each year more convinced that warring governments were evil. She yearned to report from Vietnam but had to wait until a British newspaper, the liberal *Guardian*, gave her credentials and a plane ticket to Saigon. Martha took things personally—she felt responsible for every "wounded, napalmed, amputated Vietnamese child" because the United States backed South Vietnam. Famously, she was said to scorn "all this objectivity shit" in her reporting. Sickened by what she saw as the loss of innocent life, she wrote articles so scathing that the South Vietnamese refused to renew her visa. No doubt the US government approved.

Gellhorn also held strong, pro-Israeli views about the Middle East and favored Israel in its ongoing conflict with Arab states. If Martha Gellhorn saw something that she believed was unjust, then it was decidedly wrong. She refused to look at both sides of an issue she felt passionate about. As a child, Martha had been raised on the principles of ethical culture and was an atheist, but she had two Jewish grandfathers and, after witnessing the inhumanity of Nazi death camps, an abiding love for Israel.

She equally despised Yasser Arafat, the self-appointed leader of Israel's Palestinian Arabs. Martha was quite blunt in her criticism of the Middle East's "oil Arabs" who ganged up on Israel, and the only Palestinians she liked were women. "The Muslim Arab attitude toward women is one of the reasons that Arabs remain so drearily retarded," she wrote in *The View from the Ground*, a look back at her career as a correspondent. "The chief reason is hate. These people really love to hate."

Martha Gellhorn relished life, and some would say she ran from death. She didn't accept old age with grace. She had a home in London, but as she aged, she withdrew to spend more and more time at her cottage in Wales. She surrounded herself with younger people; her favorites were young men whom she called her "chaps." She smoked unceasingly, her sand-edged voice marked by the transatlantic accent adopted by Americans who lived in Europe.

Martha Gellhorn was hell-bent on staying relevant and deeply saddened when she felt too old to cover the war in Bosnia in the early 1990s. Late in life her body betrayed her, and she developed cancer in her nose. When she started to go blind, she decided she'd had enough. In February 1998, she dressed in a yellow nightgown and climbed into her bed, made up with yellow sheets. With headphones over her ears and an audio book in her cassette player, she overdosed on sleeping pills. She was just shy of 90.

A new generation of Americans was introduced to Martha Gellhorn in a made-for-TV movie that portrayed her marriage with Ernest Hemingway. She would have hated it, although she might have grudgingly admitted that Hemingway helped her through a period of writer's block during the Spanish Civil War.

Shortly after she died, Sandy Matthews, Martha Gellhorn's stepson, gave an interview to the *Guardian* to dispute a new biography that portrayed Gellhorn with "sexual scandal-mongering and cod psychology." He'd had an affectionate relationship with her over the years, and Martha had asked him to settle her estate after she died. John Pilger, one of her "chaps" in her later years, also defended her memory, recounting how Martha, at age 75, got into her car and drove into the Welsh hills to cover a miner's strike that bitterly divided Britons.

Most of the media were then concentrating on miners' violence on the picket line, which echoed [British prime minister Margaret] Thatcher's "enemy within." She phoned me from a call box in Newbridge. "Listen," she said, "you ought to see what the police are doing here. They're surrounding villages at night and beating the hell out of people. Why isn't that being reported?" I suggested she report it. "I've done it," she replied.

Women Report in World War II, 1939–1945

The German Army invaded Poland on August 31, 1939, immediately drawing most of Europe into World War II. American reporters stayed at their posts in Berlin until the United States entered the war in December 1941.

The United States fought the war in two theaters in Europe and the Pacific. American women reporters found their way to both. Experienced correspondents such as Virginia Cowles (who wrote for the London *Sunday Times*) and Martha Gellhorn, both of whom had witnessed the Spanish Civil War, turned their attention to Germany's invasion of Poland and Czechoslovakia. Sonia Tomara, a Russian exile, and Tania Long, a naturalized American of Russian-English descent, were hired by the *New York Herald Tribune*.

Helen Kirkpatrick fought her own battle to win a spot reporting from London for the *Chicago Daily News*. In September 1940 she and her friend Ginny Cowles observed the Royal Air Force from the White Cliffs of Dover as Spitfires and Mustangs fought the Battle of Britain. They both endured the Blitz in London when the German *Luftwaffe* dropped bombs night after night on Britain's cities.

There were others in Europe: Ruth Cowan, Eleanor Packard, May Craig, Ann Stringer, Patricia Lochridge, Marjorie Avery,

Photographer Therese Bonney became a comic book hero during World War II. *Library of Congress LC-USZC4-9007*

Catherine Coyne, and Betty Murphy Phillips, the nation's first African American war correspondent, who had the bad luck to get sick before she had a chance to get to the front. Four had cameras: Toni Frissell, a high-fashion photographer for *Vogue* and *Harper's Bazaar*; the flamboyant Lee Miller, also of *Vogue*; Therese Bonney, who focused on the plight of children and adults left homeless by war; and *Life* magazine's Margaret Bourke-White.

Later, American women gained credentials from the US Navy to cover the fight against Japan. As the Battle of Iwo Jima unfolded in the Pacific in 1945, Patricia Lochridge and photographer Dickey Chapelle worked aboard hospital ships. Old-timer Peggy Hull reported from a land-based hospital on the island of Saipan.

Margaret Bourke-White

REPORTING FROM MOSCOW, TUNIS, AND BUCHENWALD

We climbed over the rail and into lifeboat No. 12. Even though we knew the torpedo splash was there, it was a shock to find ourselves sitting in water up to our waists. As we started slowly downward, I hugged my musette bag to my chest, hoping to keep my camera dry.— Margaret Bourke-White

"Wait," Father said, and then in a rush the blackness was broken by a sudden magic of flowing metal and flying sparks. I can hardly describe my joy. To me at that age, a foundry represented the beginning and end of all beauty.

Pure joy. That visit to the foundry to watch the first steps in building a printing press was a treasured memory for Margaret White. She cherished those few hours when her father, a brilliant but distant man, came out of his usual trance and paid attention to her. Joseph White was an inventor who happily spent most of his waking hours pondering the best way to design printing presses and glorious color images.

While Father "thought," Margaret's mother, Minnie Bourke White, busied herself with her three children, partly to keep them from distracting Father and partly because Minnie White raised her children to be fearless. Together they explored the wide outdoors, and Margaret returned home with masses of pollywog eggs and leaves to feed the hundreds of caterpillars that lived on a dining room windowsill. A budding herpetologist, she kept a menagerie of pet turtles and snakes, including a baby boa constrictor that lived in a blanket and a "plump and harmless puff adder." (Margaret never explained why that puff adder, a deadly, venomous snake, was "harmless.")

When Joseph White broke away from mulling over his latest patents, the family took outings and vacations. When Margaret was a little girl in the early 1900s, amateur photography was a novelty among American consumers. Always the inventor, Joseph White played around with camera lenses and 3-D images; he was fascinated with how light played through lenses, prisms, cameras, and projectors. For those who could not see at all, Joe White invented the first Braille printing press.

Margaret didn't think she fit in with the other girls at Plainfield High School in New Jersey. Inner-directed, she had a strict conscience and far more self-control than others her age. Her mother had taught her never to take the easy way out of anything and to always tell the truth, and Margaret didn't question being punished even for childish carelessness. Margaret and her sister had to be content with wearing cotton stockings when the other girls wore silk, and colorful Sunday funnies were yanked from newspapers before they read them.

Margaret adored dancing, and though she had plenty of boys around for picnics, canoe trips, and steak roasts, she never was asked to dance at school parties. When she took the top literary prize her sophomore year, she still stood neglected at the dance that followed, a dejected and dismal wallflower until an older girl volunteered to dance with her. Margaret was sure the older girl felt the same way she did, "that we both could be stricken invisible."

Margaret enrolled to study art at Columbia University in New York City. Though she was unaware of it then, it was a stroke of luck when she signed up for a weekly two-hour photography class with Clarence H. White (no relation), whose innovative images were the talk of the avant-garde. Professor White and his crowd of protégés strove to elevate photography as an art form at a time when critics relegated "art" to painters, sculptors, and architects.

Margaret wasn't especially interested in taking pictures, but White's class offered her a chance to explore design and composition in a new medium. What was more, she took the class while nursing a broken heart; her beloved father had died during Christmas break. Sometime thereafter, Margaret's mother bought her a camera, a 3¼-by-4¼-inch Ica Reflex, modeled after the much pricier Graflex camera. At $20, the Ica still was a costly purchase for her mother, and Margaret's new camera came with a cracked lens.

Margaret set her camera aside as she pursued new paths in her education. She moved on to Rutgers University for the summer session and then to the University of Michigan for the fall term. There she met a tall, attractive graduate student named Everett Chapman. "Chappie" saw Margaret as they passed through a revolving door and wouldn't stop circling until she said yes to a date.

Margaret the wallflower had begun to bloom. It was love at first sight for her and Chappie, and they married quickly. Chappie planned to teach at Purdue University as Margaret resumed her studies, now in herpetology.

Their marriage was short-lived, thanks to an unbroken "silver-cord entanglement" that held Chappie to his mother. The elder Mrs. Chapman had wept all through his marriage ceremony to Margaret. Chappie departed for Ann Arbor, Michigan, and left them both at the family cabin. Mrs. Chapman took advantage of his absence to tell Margaret—through a wall— "You got him away from me. I congratulate you. I never want to see you again."

Margaret left and walked the 17 miles to Ann Arbor to find Chappie, thinking that would make things right. However, though they loved each other, neither Chappie nor Margaret had the life experience to deal with his dominating mother. Their marriage lasted two years, until Margaret left Chappie and went back to school.

By now Margaret had attended six different colleges, and her interests ran wide. She had studied art, herpetology, and paleontology. For her senior year she picked Cornell University in upstate New York, attracted to its lovely photos of waterfalls and Cayuga Lake. Just about penniless, she enrolled in the fall of 1926 to study biology, planning to get a job to help pay her expenses. But jobs were gone by the time Margaret arrived in Ithaca, so she picked up her camera. With such scenery all around, she thought, surely she could sell her photographs, and for a time she did, as holiday gifts.

Margaret got her marketing lesson when sales dried up in January and she was left with piles of her photos on her dorm room floor. She found a different customer, this time Cornell's *Alumni Review*, where her shots appeared on the cover. When Cornell alumni advised Margaret to become an architectural photographer, they "opened a dazzling new vista," and she made herself a plan.

Margaret graduated and took the Great Lakes night boat from Buffalo, New York, to Cleveland, Ohio, her legal residence. She went to the courthouse, got her divorce, and took back her maiden name, adding a hyphen between "Bourke" and "White."

Margaret started her photography business in the Flats of Cleveland, a gritty industrial area along the Cuyahoga River. She didn't mind the dirt and stench of mills and was captivated by "smokestacks on the upper rim of the Flats rais[ing] their smoking arms over the blast furnaces, where ore meets coke and becomes steel." She longed to get inside to photograph the fires and sparks and giant cauldrons of molten metal. But steel mills were no place for a woman, she was told, and it took weeks before she was permitted to enter one. First she had to prove herself.

Margaret befriended a kindly camera shop owner, Alfred Hall Bemis, who became her mentor. He helped her build a developing lab in her apartment, shared all kinds of technical advice, and taught her that it was easy to make a "million technicians but not photographers." When competition showed up, "Beme" counseled Margaret, "Don't worry about what the other fellow is doing. Shoot off your own guns."

With hard work, talent, and the "luck" that came after endless rounds of picture taking and networking, Margaret finally got into the Cleveland mills. She faced long weeks of technical problems, because the mills' cavelike interiors, lit only by the glowing blast furnaces, played all sorts of light tricks on the camera lens. Margaret experimented this way and that until she got the shots she was looking for. Her girlhood fascination with flowing metal and flying sparks blazed in her photographs of stark, raw beauty. In the next two decades, Margaret Bourke-White earned her reputation as one of the nation's most skilled photographers. In 1929, she was hired to take photos for a brand-new project, *Fortune* magazine, the weekly brainchild of a young New York publisher named Henry Luce, who had launched *Time* magazine four years earlier. *Fortune* lived true to its name, highlighting the news of American business and industry where "pictures and words should be conscious partners." Luce had spotted Margaret's compelling photographs of the Cleveland mills, and he expected her to bring the same eye for detail to her work at *Fortune*.

Margaret's spare, black-and-white photographs captured American industry in a novel way. She saw industrial products as objects of beauty. Giant pieces of machinery, electrical lines, tiny watch parts, a row of perfectly positioned plow blades—all of these were worthy subjects for Margaret's cameras.

Architectural photography continued to intrigue her. As the wind blew through Manhattan's streets in the winter of 1929–30, she photographed the rise of New York's Chrysler Building, a steel-shelled ode to Art Nouveau beauty. Margaret herself was portrayed in a famous photo when she crawled out her studio window onto one of the building's steel gargoyles, 800 feet above the ground, to take a picture.

Though the United States was deep into the Great Depression, Luce launched yet another magazine in 1936, this one called *Life*, a large-size weekly that featured more pictures than words. Margaret shot its first cover photo, of the massive concrete Fort Peck Dam, which appeared on November 23, 1936. The shot reminded readers of an imposing Egyptian temple, but this was an American achievement, revered as a marvel of Yankee engineering.

But the despair of the Depression now overwhelmed Americans as no national crisis ever had. On assignment for *Fortune* in 1934, Margaret flew to Omaha, Nebraska, to photograph the Dust Bowl, dried-up farmland than ran from North Dakota all the way south to the Texas panhandle. Her pilot ferried her in a beat-up, two-seat Curtiss Robin, and they crash-landed on Margaret's final day of shooting. She took the crash in stride when she thought back to the bleakness she'd seen from the air. The land was a "ghostly patchwork of half-buried corn, and . . . rivers of sand." Its human occupants tore at her heart: "They had no defense and no plan. They were numbed like their own dumb animals, and many of these animals were choking, dying in drifting soil."

Something new rose up in Margaret's soul. She began to think of people as subjects for her camera. "Here in the Dakotas with these farmers, I saw everything in a new light. How could I tell it all in pictures? Here were faces engraved with the very paralysis of despair."

In the midst of a very successful career taking pictures for advertising agencies and doing magazine work, Margaret took a different path. She agreed to collaborate on a book with an author named Erskine Caldwell, who had made the headlines with his book, *Tobacco Road*, about southern sharecroppers who led lives of desperation and depravity. Caldwell wanted to prove that *Tobacco Road* was a realistic portrayal of sharecropping, and he needed photographs to help him do that.

Not sure at first whether they liked each other, Margaret and Erskine took off on a road trip through the Deep South and, somewhere along the line, fell in love. Erskine Caldwell, Georgia-bred, taught Margaret about his southern ways. Margaret grew both personally and professionally as she realized that a photographer must put "more heart and mind into his preparation that will ever show in any photograph." Her portraits of weathered, beaten women and men in *You Have Seen Their Faces* reflected her maturity as an artist when it was published in 1937. She and Erskine Caldwell married two years later.

World War II engulfed Europe in 1939, and Margaret's work for *Life* took her to far-flung spots. Her *Life* editor, Wilson Hicks, had a hunch that the new peace pact signed by Germany and the Soviet Union would not hold, and Hicks predicted that Germans and Russians would go to war. Hicks was correct; Hitler declared war against the Soviets in June 1941. Margaret was dispatched to Moscow to take pictures at the Eastern Front.

Germany had conquered most of Europe from the Atlantic to the Russian border, so Margaret and Erskine got to Russia via a backdoor route—just as Bessie Beatty, Rheta Childe Dorr, and Peggy Hull had in 1917. Instead of riding the slow-moving Trans-Siberian Railway, Margaret and Erskine hopped on a series of small planes to fly across China and Inner Mongolia and entered Russia through Alma-Ata (today's Almaty, Kazakhstan). Margaret was impressed by the number of statues and monuments dedicated to the Russian premier, Joseph Stalin.

On July 22, 1941, the Germans launched air attacks on Moscow. Margaret was the only foreign news photographer in the city, ready to clinch the scoop of her life as German bombs rained down on Moscow rooftops. But the Russians had issued an *ukase*—an edict—forbidding use of cameras, and civilians were ordered to underground shelters to wait out air raids. Margaret figured she could work around the ban on cameras, and she planned to stay above ground during bombings.

From her hotel balcony stretched Moscow's most famous view: the Kremlin, the onion-shaped domes of St. Basil's Cathedral, Vladimir Lenin's tomb, and Red Square. There Margaret placed four cameras, set on timed exposure, to capture the streaks of light that swept to the ground as the bombs fell. Russian blackout wardens made frequent checks of hotel rooms searching for lawbreakers like her, and Margaret rolled under her bed when she heard them coming. Bending over her bathtub, she developed her film in trays and hung the negatives on cords strung across the bathroom pipes and pinned to the edges of towels and curtains. Her negatives found their way into diplomatic bags that traveled from the American embassy safely out of Russia and into *Life*'s New York offices.

Margaret had another plan to photograph Joseph Stalin, but the mysterious "Man of Steel" seemed unreachable until President Roosevelt's personal envoy, Harry Hopkins, stepped in to help. Hopkins negotiated with Russian foreign minister Vyacheslav Molotov to get Margaret access to the stone-faced Stalin.

Margaret prepared for this prized photo session with great care. Americans wanted to know, was this man really in charge of Soviet Russia, or was he just a figurehead? She did her best to get Stalin to relax as she set up her cameras and arranged the lighting in his Kremlin office. She sized Stalin up and decided there was nothing superhuman about him. She was five feet five, and Stalin was shorter. This small man with the pockmarked face was a nobody. Margaret's snap judgment of Stalin paralleled Dorothy Thompson's initial take on Adolf Hitler back in 1934. And like Thompson, she needed to look again and changed her mind. "Then in the next minute, I decided there was nothing insignificant about Stalin. . . . One look at that granite face, and I was sure that Stalin made all the decisions."

Stalin's face was a block of ice, and no amount of small talk could make him change his expression. The nervous Margaret spilled a pocketful of peanut flashbulbs, and they went bouncing on the floor. She dropped to her knees to gather them up, and Stalin started to laugh. Margaret rushed to her camera and managed to make two exposures before the strong man's face turned back to stone. She left thinking that this was the "most determined, the most ruthless personality" she'd ever met.

As Margaret grew ever more valuable to *Life* and took assignments far and wide, she put her life with Erskine Caldwell on hold. Promises of work in Hollywood led him in one direction as Margaret chose another. Margaret was on the move, far too independent to settle down. A Hollywood existence, or the promise of a new home in Arizona with Erskine, seemed like "golden chains" to Margaret, and she and Erskine went their separate ways. The marriage lasted three years until they divorced, amicably, in 1942.

With the backing of *Life*, Margaret was credentialed as a war photojournalist with the US Army Air Forces in 1942. The Army War College designed her uniform along the lines of what officers wore, adding a skirt. Gold buttons ran up her jacket front, and her shoulders bore the insignia of a war correspondent. An outdoor outfitter named Abercrombie & Fitch made Margaret's first uniform. Smartly turned out, she and other correspondents dined in the officers' mess and held the rank of captain, though they couldn't collect an officer's pay unless they were captured.

On to England Margaret flew, where she lived at a secret bomber base that was home to B-17s, the mighty Flying Fortresses. An aircrew asked her to name their plane, and she chose *Flying Flit Gun,* which they painted on the Fortress along with a bug sprayer and three insects with the faces of Hitler, Mussolini, and Hirohito. It pleased Margaret to see "Peggy" (her nickname) painted on the No. 3 engine, a special honor usually reserved for fiancées and wives, when she christened the *Flying Flit Gun* with a bottle of Coke.

After war reporters got the go-ahead to fly on bombing runs over Germany, Margaret stood in line to wait her turn. But an unseen force denied her permission, and matters worsened when the first two reporters left on a bombing raid and only one returned. Margaret chafed at the "invisible ink" that kept her from doing her job. She was a seasoned photojournalist, a mature adult nearly twice as old as many of the fighting men she wanted to photograph.

Her problem was typical of women reporters who tried to get in on the action during World War II. Most military commanders didn't want women anywhere near the line of battle, on an aircraft, or even aboard ships. Having a woman around would only distract fighting men from their work.

Whispers on base told Margaret that the Allies were about to invade North Africa to force out the German Army and its *Luftwaffe* (air force). Margaret repeated her request one evening

Margaret Bourke-White's photos brought despicable images of Nazi death camps home to Americans. *Holocaust Museum*

when General Jimmy Doolittle, commander of the Eighth Air Force, walked into the officers' lounge. Margaret had met Doolittle years before at the Indianapolis Motor Speedway, and his wife Jo had embroidered Margaret's name on a tablecloth filled with signatures of their friends. Jimmy Doolittle wouldn't say no, of that Margaret was sure. She was assigned to a berth on a ship crossing the Mediterranean, though. The Allies weren't about to let a woman fly—that was too dangerous.

Ironically, the so-called safe passage turned into a nightmare when German submarines attacked the convoy. Margaret's ship was torpedoed, and hundreds of soldiers, sailors, nurses, and a few members of the Women's Army Corps (WACS) crawled over the ship's side and descended down swirling nets into lifeboats. Margaret's description of the attack in her autobiography, *Portrait of Myself*, offered one of the best memoirs from the war about how it felt to be in a rudderless lifeboat as people died around her. Some of the 6,000 soldiers on board had been trapped; others drowned. Yet even then, spots of humor shone through. ("Hi, taxi!" called one survivor in the water, as she flagged down a lifeboat.) All the while, Margaret hugged her one camera, tucked into her musette bag, to her chest. She lost four others when her ship was scuttled to the bottom of the sea.

Margaret Bourke-White had escaped from a torpedoed ship, and so the commanders had no more excuses to keep her off an airplane. She prepared thoroughly and planned how she would maneuver her heavy equipment around the tightly packed bomber, filled as it was with wires and tubes and a load of bombs stacked like books on shelves. She donned her flying suit, dressing in fleece-lined leather pants and jacket, heavy boots, and electric mittens to wear at altitude—15,000 feet for a B-17, which had no heat. The aircraft was unpressurized as well, which meant little or no oxygen at that altitude. Margaret practiced with her portable oxygen bottle, knowing she had no more than four minutes to rove free from the permanent oxygen line the crew depended on.

On January 22, 1943, Margaret flew in the lead airplane in formation across the North African desert that would attack a German airfield in Tunis, Tunisia. When the B-17 crossed into enemy airspace, she took photos as the bombardier removed the safety pins that secured each bomb should they crash in friendly territory. Pop, pop, went her flashbulbs, not what the bombardier expected. "Jesus Christ, they're exploding in my hands," he cried through the plane's intercom. The shaken airman had forgotten that Margaret was on his plane. Later, Margaret declared that the incident proved her point—women were no distraction around men who did dangerous work.

As the airplane flew its bomb run over its target, Margaret leaned past a machine gun and into the left waist window to take pictures through a few chinks of open space. The captain bobbed and weaved the Fortress to evade the antiaircraft fire coming from ack-ack guns on the ground. As the plane dipped and rolled, Margaret shot her pictures, some of them straight down. The *Flying Flit Gun* took two hits in the wing, but the sturdy Fortress, commanded by lead pilot Major Paul Tibbets, made it safely home to an airbase on an oasis named "Garden of Allah."

Neither Margaret nor Paul Tibbets, a quiet, unassuming man, knew that the young pilot had a fateful mission ahead of him. On August 6, 1945, Paul Tibbets would sit in the left seat of the *Enola Gay* and drop an atomic bomb on Hiroshima, Japan.

Six months later, Margaret returned to North Africa to the very airfield they had bombed, now under Allied control. Margaret was on her way to Italy, the "soft underbelly" of Europe, where the Allies had launched an attack and planned to drive north. As she waited for a flight, she wandered into a graveyard across from the airfield. She was "caught up sharp" when she saw a graveyard marked with painted swastikas that were dated January 22, 1943—the day she'd flown on that mission. For a moment "those clumsy wooden swastikas took away the impersonality of war and recalled a day when death rained from the skies."

Margaret spent five months on the Italian Front taking pictures from tiny, defenseless Piper Cubs as they flew reconnaissance across the lines of battle. She took more at a field hospital when the Germans attacked it, sending Screaming Meemies into their compound. The shelling was terrifying, the dreaded "sound of rushing wind from the mountains," that built into a swell of sound, then a scream, then the roar of an explosion. One hit the hospital mess tent just 30 feet from where Margaret and a group of nurses had flung themselves on the ground. She took lots of pictures that night, as surgeons and nurses worked on the wounded. Everywhere, everyone was donating blood—truck drivers, ambulance crews, hospital staff, and gun crews, when they could make it in from the front. It was a "grotesque routine" of work, then diving for the floor, then back up to work some more.

The terror of that night was to be only a memory. When Margaret returned to *Life's* offices, Wilson Hicks gave her the bad news. Her precious negatives of the hospital, the brave nurses and doctors, a dying soldier who had asked for watermelon, the truck drivers donating blood, were lost somewhere in the Pentagon. They never turned up. Another 300 photos that Margaret took during the army's push northward through snow and ice were stolen from an army jeep. War could explain a lot, Margaret realized, but carelessness was unforgiveable.

Margaret left Italy and arrived at the front on Germany's Rhine River in time to travel with General George Patton's

Third Army. She thought of Nazi Germany's last days in 1945 as a *Götterdämmerung*—(the German term for "the twilight of the gods," the violent, chaotic downfall of an empire). Margaret was with Patton when he inspected Buchenwald, a Nazi concentration camp, after the American Army liberated it on April 11, 1945. Patton was so angry when he inspected the camp, where more than 56,000 prisoners had died, that he ordered his military police to round up 1,000 German men and women who lived in nearby Weimar and force them to see for themselves the unspeakable evidence of Nazi brutality.

The MPs were so angry they brought in 2,000 Weimar residents and forced them to look at the piles of bodies stuffed into sheds, the burnt remains of others still in the cremation ovens, the mass graves of the dead, and the living skeletons of the men and boys who had somehow survived. The Germans claimed ignorance, denying it all. "We didn't know. We didn't know," Margaret wrote, quoting everyday Germans dressed in shirts and ties and housedresses. "But they did know."

Margaret moved on to photograph another labor camp where, only hours before, German SS guards had burned the inmates to death in the mess hall before running away. The bodies were still smoldering. The few who escaped, Margaret noted bitterly, ran into a meadow, only to be shot by boys in the Hitler Youth. For Margaret, the dead in the meadow, who had come so close to freedom, "made the most heartbreaking sight of all."

Margaret pulled a "veil" over her mind as she took pictures at Buchenwald, working methodically and grateful that the camera placed a barrier between her and the horror she beheld. Two of her photos ran in *Life* on May 7 along with the work of several other photojournalists who recorded the atrocities, a black-and-white record that proved rumors about Nazi barbarism were true and not the work of anti-German propaganda. Many more weren't published until 1960 when *Life* ran a special double issue, "25 Years of *Life*." Her shot of 15 Buchenwald survivors leaning on a wire fence, heads shaved and eyes hollow, became one of her best known.

After the war, Margaret Bourke-White kept taking pictures. She went to India and patiently waited to photograph Mohandas Gandhi, the Hindu leader who used civil disobedience to gain India's independence from Great Britain. The mystical Gandhi insisted that Margaret learn to use a spinning wheel before he permitted her to take only three photos of him. After taking two shots, Margaret knew she hadn't gotten what she had come for, but her third and final try resulted in a masterpiece. Gandhi was assassinated soon thereafter, and Margaret's pictures of his funeral also ran in *Life*.

Margaret went on to take pictures of abused diamond miners in South Africa and also covered the Korean War. She developed Parkinson's disease in her mid-40s and fought its crippling effects for the next 20 years as it incapacitated her muscles and nerves. She died in 1971.

4

A Cold War
1945–1989

The Allied victory in World War II placed part of Germany and all of Eastern Europe into the hands of the Soviet Union. By 1947, the Iron Curtain had fallen across Europe, dividing it into democratic and Communist nations. For the next 50 years, the Cold War mentality underscored how nations did business.

The Cold War created a sense of anxiety among Americans, despite the country's booming economy and status as the leading nation of the Free World. Even as Americans feared a nuclear war with the "Reds," the United States made giant strides in war technology, developing B-52s and missiles to carry hydrogen bombs to wipe out enemy targets. The Soviets did the same.

A rabidly anti-Communist senator, Joseph McCarthy, was trying to convince the public that "Commies" were destroying the American way of life and conducted hearings that appeared on television. Children in schools practiced air-raid drills and crawled under their desks. The United States and the USSR embarked on a space race after Russia launched the first satellite into orbit in 1957. Overseas, the United States tasked its military and the newly formed Central Intelligence Agency (CIA) with ensuring that other nations, large and small, stay in line with the Free World.

The Cold War never turned hot between the United States and Soviet Russia, but the two nations equipped and financed small wars and revolutions in Africa, Asia, and Central and South America. When the Cuban Revolution put Fidel Castro in power in 1959, it soon became clear that Communists had a foothold in the Americas. Castro's presence in Cuba seemed to signal imminent revolution all across Latin America and the Caribbean, and for the next 25 years, the United States bolstered anti-Communist governments, regimes that nonetheless were decidedly nondemocratic.

With China under the control of its Communist rulers by 1949, the US government feared that all of East Asia could also go "red." When Communist North Korea invaded South Korea in 1950, the United States rushed to aid the South and fought an undeclared war against North Korea and China. At the US Department of Defense, a theory in foreign policy began to take hold: that once a small country succumbed to Communist rule, its neighbors would fall like a series of dominoes. This domino theory became the operating principle for American foreign policy during the Cold War years in the 1950s and '60s, driving the buildup of US forces to fight the Vietnam War.

Marguerite Higgins

REPORTING FROM DACHAU AND SEOUL

Then suddenly, for the first time in the war, I experienced the cold, awful certainty that there was no escape. My reactions were trite. As with most people who suddenly accept death as inevitable and imminent, I was simply filled with surprise that this was finally going to happen to me.—Marguerite Higgins

Sometimes the men and women who report the news become news themselves. Celebrity journalists are nothing new in American culture; Elizabeth Cochrane, aka Nellie Bly, captured readers' imaginations in 1889 with her globetrotting exploits, and Peggy Hull drew quite a following as the girl reporter "who got to Paris." But none rose faster nor further than Marguerite Higgins, a war correspondent for the *New York Herald Tribune*, when she went to Korea to report on the Chinese invasion in June 1950, which won her a Pulitzer Prize for international reporting in 1951. Her friend Carl Mydans, a prominent *Life* magazine photographer, shot a series of pictures and wrote a flattering article that *Life* ran in a six-page spread on October 2, 1950. Marguerite Higgins became a national sensation.

Mydans's story neatly summed up how Maggie was "engaged in three separate campaigns" in Korea: one to report on the war; the second, her famous feud with fellow *Herald Tribune* reporter Homer Bigart; and the third, "ever to deny that sex has anything to do with war correspondence." In fact, Maggie's dear friend (and defender) was spot on about her life as a war reporter, and biographers and students of American history and culture have wrangled over the details of her life ever since.

Marguerite Higgins seemed to know what she wanted from life. She cultivated an air of cool detachment, though she claimed to have deep doubts about how she measured up against everyone else. Born in Hong Kong in 1920 to an American father and French mother, she grew up speaking a mix of languages and was teased about her accent when her family moved to Oakland, California. Her father, Lawrence Higgins, like so many well-heeled businessmen, lost his job as a stockbroker when the stock market crashed in October 1929. Though he found other work, Marguerite's dissolute father succumbed to alcoholism that put a strain on his family. Maggie's mother, Marguerite Goddard Higgins, got a job teaching French at a tony girls' school where her daughter could attend tuition-free.

Marguerite's father resented the life that the Depression had doled out to him, complaining about the "flabby routine of his petite bourgeois life in Oakland, California," to use his wife's French words for the lower middle class. He spoke to his daughter of his heroic past during World War I, first as an ambulance driver and later as a pilot, and pointedly raised his daughter to fear nothing and no one. Years later, after Maggie had made a splash as a war correspondent, he told a *Time* interviewer that he raised Maggie so "that she should always be able to stand on her own feet." Then Lawrence Higgins said something else:

> Marguerite is not so much competitive, as she is a perfectionist. There was only one place for Marguerite and that was the top, regardless as of what she was doing . . . learning to swim, to play the violin, or whatever she went into. But it was strictly for her own satisfaction, not to beat somebody else out.

From the girls' school, Maggie went to college at the University of California at Berkeley. She joined a sorority, where she must have shocked a few sisters when she stated she believed in free love. But on large parts of Berkeley's campus, the "petite bourgeois" attitudes of Oakland didn't fly. Her interests turned to working for the campus paper, the *Daily Californian*. Big ideas were always churning at Berkeley, and Maggie met students and professors who didn't share the same values as her neighbors at home. She mingled with liberals and Socialists who dreamed about a new and different order to American society, and she dated a Communist, a philosophy student named Stanley Moore who was studying for a doctorate.

For a time Maggie worked as a cub reporter for a small-town paper, but the promise of working in big-time journalism lured her to the master's program at the Columbia University Graduate School of Journalism in New York. Only 12 slots were open to women when Maggie applied, and she scrambled to get a spot just four days before classes began in the fall of 1941. Off to New York Maggie went, rooming with an artist in Greenwich Village, where bohemian culture flourished.

While she attended grad school, Maggie worked as a stringer for the *New York Herald Tribune*, then a leading city paper and fierce competitor against the *New York Times*. She dug around Columbia's campus for stories and submitted them to the *Herald Tribune*, which paid her only for the ones they accepted. At some point during her studies she announced that she planned to become more famous than Dorothy Thompson, then the nation's leading female journalist.

Maggie's talent for digging out news got her a full-time job at the *Herald Tribune* after she graduated in 1942, and she began the typical climb up the reporter's ladder—first on general assignments, next on district news, then the graveyard shift reporting on crime and fires, then to the rewrite desk, and finally to the top as a features writer. Maggie never did become a top-notch writer among American journalists, but several old-timers noticed that no one could equal her skill at getting news, including fresh angles to old stories.

It was a man's world in the city room at the *New York Herald Tribune*, even if a handful of women like Maggie Higgins worked there. After hours, a reporter was likely to stroll down the street to the Artists and Writers Restaurant, affectionately called "Bleecks" (pronounced "Blake's") after its owner. Over drinks at the bar or in the back room, newspapermen talked shop and tossed around ideas, much as executives and managers at New York's banks and corporate headquarters gathered in their private dining rooms for drinks and lunch. Maggie Higgins wasn't welcome in that back room, as women in general were excluded from these sacred male watering holes where they talked shop and made important decisions. Maggie may have considered herself as competent as any male reporter and entitled to the same information, but in the 1940s, most men didn't see things that way.

Controversy and gossip followed Maggie Higgins from her college years onward. Her outward appearance—bright blue eyes, tall, athletic figure, and curly blond hair—could easily have attracted others. But the simple truth was that most people, women or men, didn't like Marguerite Higgins. Her single-mindedness and her need for perfection worked against her. But Maggie didn't care what other people thought. Her raw ambition made her few friends and many enemies. Soon enough, the gossip began: that she stole colleagues' stories and that she slept with sources, editors, and other reporters, all in her drive to reach the top and stay there.

With America at war in two theaters of operations, Maggie Higgins ached to get overseas as a correspondent. Seeing her wish granted didn't seem likely; there were plenty of experienced, hardened men at the *Herald Tribune* who were readily credentialed by the War Department to work in combat zones, including another Californian named John Steinbeck (who went on to become a leading novelist and Pulitzer Prize winner, as Maggie would).

In late 1944, Maggie Higgins got to Europe and soon found her way to the *Herald Tribune's* Paris bureau where her skilled French gave her an edge in reporting. Over the fall and winter that year, as the Allies made their final push into Germany and Austria, she traveled with the US Third Army commanded by General George Patton. She got to know lots of military men—from troops on the ground to top brass—and she made enemies. Some of the other women correspondents, some 20 or more years older than Maggie (who was 24), resented her untidiness. She showed no regard for the older women's standing or experience. She ignored the smudges of carbon paper on her face and wore her uniform with tennis shoes. Worst were the rumors that Maggie Higgins would sleep with a military man or another reporter in exchange for information.

Whatever others may have thought, Maggie earned her editors' respect and was rewarded for her reporting when the *Herald Tribune* named her its Berlin bureau chief in 1947. She covered the transformation of Poland from a republic to a Communist society after the Iron Curtain dropped on Europe, and she watched the Berlin Airlift take off in 1948.

Tongues continued to wag about Marguerite Higgins in Berlin, where she fell in love with a married man, General William Hall. More gossip followed; there was a new book out at home with the provocative title, *Shriek with Pleasure*, written by Toni Howard, another woman reporter who knew Maggie in Berlin. Its protagonist very much resembled Maggie Higgins, and the plot was a "bitchy little story," according to Keyes Beech of the *Chicago Daily News*, who worked with Maggie later. When she was transferred to Tokyo as bureau chief in 1950, it looked like a big step back for Maggie, and some in her circle quietly cheered. Maggie arrived in April to find Tokyo life quiet and boring—until there was a surprise attack in a neighboring country. On Sunday, June 25, 1950, the North Korean People's Army, backed by Communist China, crossed over the 38th parallel in a full-court offensive against South Korea. That afternoon, Maggie Higgins showed up at the Haneda airfield to fly to Korea. Three other newsmen were there: Beech of the *Chicago Daily News*, Burton Crane of the *New York Times*, and Frank Gibney of *Time*. Gibney suggested that "Korea was no place for a woman," but Maggie ignored him. After several false starts and a side trip to southern Japan, they found room on an empty C-54 cargo plane that was to return filled with Americans evacuating Seoul. The pilot was amazed that the four didn't plan to come back with him.

From Kimpo (now Gimpo) Airfield, where grounded planes were on fire, the four reporters hurried on to Seoul where American military advisors worked and lived. Clearly, South Korea was in chaos, as streams of refugees poured into Seoul from the north, just 35 miles away. Maggie recalled the scene thusly:

> The road to Seoul was crowded with refugees. There were hundreds of Korean women with babies bound papoose-style to their backs and huge bundles on their heads. There were scores of trucks, elaborately camouflaged with branches. . . .
>   It was a moving and rather terrifying experience, there on that rainy road to Seoul, to have the crowds cheer and wave as our little caravan of Americans went by. . . . I

thought then, as I was to think often in later days, I hope we don't let them down.

The South Koreans fought well but were no match for the Russian-made tanks that ground their way along the Uijeongbu corridor toward Seoul. Late in the night, Maggie—relegated to separate sleeping quarters at American headquarters and separated from the other reporters—was called to evacuate along with American soldiers and move south toward a bridge that crossed the Han River. She watched as the bridge exploded into orange flames. It had been destroyed by the disorganized South Koreans in a defensive move to keep the Communists from moving closer. But the South Koreans had miscalculated their timing, leaving thousands of their own soldiers and citizens— and the Americans—trapped on the north bank of the Han. There seemed to be no other way across the river.

In the midst of retreat, an American colonel pointed out to Maggie that she could file a story from a nearby radio truck. She grabbed her typewriter,

> put it on the front of the jeep, and typed furiously. Streams of retreating South Korean soldiers were then passing our stationary convoy. Many of them turned their heads and gaped at the sight of an American woman, dressed in a navy-blue skirt, flowered blouse, and bright blue sweater, typing away on a jeep in the haze of daybreak. I got my copy all right. But as far as I know, communications never were established long enough to send it.

The Americans commandeered tiny boats and began to push across the river, pointing rifles at anyone who threatened them. It was havoc all around as people tried to escape. Korean soldiers shot at fleeing boatmen, hoping they would return to shore so they could escape as well. Others stormed the smaller craft and swamped them as they climbed in. Maggie was separated from the other reporters, and she crossed the Han River safely. A single file of refugees then marched up a mountain trail toward Suwon, South Korea's brand new temporary capital. The group included the Korean minister of the interior, South Korean soldiers, an old man, diplomats, children, and Maggie Higgins.

In the opening assaults of the Korean War, Maggie and the other reporters witnessed—and lived through—four evacuations in 10 days. Maggie saw the very first American death in that war, as 19-year-old Private Kenneth Shadrick lifted his head to take aim and was shot. The reporters could only shake their heads, knowing that these young soldiers had just finished basic training and had no real battle experience. Outnumbered and green, these young men and their commanders had sacrificed themselves. "Are you correspondents telling the people back home the truth?" a 26-year-old lieutenant barked at Maggie. "Are you telling them that out of one platoon of 20 men, we have three left? Are you telling them that we have nothing to fight with, and that it is an utterly useless war?" Maggie did, in a book she titled simply, *War in Korea: The Report of a Woman Combat Correspondent.*

If Maggie had held communist sympathies during college, she abandoned them when she reported on the Korean War:

> We know now that it is fortunate for our world that it resisted Red aggression at that time and in that place. Korea has served as a kind of international alarm clock to wake up the world.
>
> There is a dangerous gap between the mobilized might of the free world and the armaments of the Red

world—the Red world which, since 1945, has been talking peace and rushing preparations for war. Korea ripped away our complacency, our smug feeling that all we had to do for our safety was to build bigger atomic bombs. Korea has shown how weak America was. It has shown how desperately we needed to arm and to produce tough, hard-fighting foot soldiers. It was better to find this out in Korea and in June of 1950 than on our own shores and possibly too late.

In the midst of trying to dodge gunfire, evacuate, write stories, and file them on time—yet another challenge—Maggie had problems of her own. Homer Bigart arrived in Korea and pulled rank on Maggie, ordering her to go back to Tokyo. Maggie protested: there was plenty of work for them both. But then Bigart got nasty and threatened to get her fired.

Bigart also told Maggie that she didn't have a single friend in Tokyo, which both puzzled and bothered her. She wondered what was going on. She learned later that four other news bureau chiefs in Seoul, the so-called "Palace Guard," who alone had access to General Douglas MacArthur, were furious when she broke the story about American bombings north of the 38th parallel. The four had agreed to release the news together at a later date and now believed that Maggie had gotten the privileged information from MacArthur himself. Maggie insisted she knew nothing of the agreement but she did know about the bombings—from a completely different source.

As Homer Bigart continued to harass Maggie, she sent a message to the bosses in New York asking permission to stay on. Days later, when she still had no answer back, she worried about what to do. She sought out her friend Carl Mydans, the *Time* and *Life* magazine photographer, to share her worries. Mydans asked her a piercing question: "What is more important to you, Maggie, the experience of covering the Korean War or fears of losing your job?"

Maggie Higgins stayed on in Korea. In mid-July, as she covered the Battle of Taejon in a jeep scrounged by Keyes Beech, Maggie got a rude shock of her own. The army was expelling her from Korea. She wrote that the news felt as though she'd been hit by gunfire. She was ordered out of the Korean theater of war immediately, and no one could explain why.

Tensions between army brass and war correspondents had arisen in Korea. It looked as though MacArthur's headquarters thought the press was more hindrance than help to their war effort. Maggie thought that MacArthur's press chief viewed the press corps as natural enemies. Correspondents were allowed use of the telephone only in the dead of night. It didn't matter if the line was free of other military traffic during waking hours. The only sure way a reporter could file her stories was to have them flown to Tokyo.

I had already been with the troops three weeks. Now, with an entire division in the line and more due to arrive, the worst had already been endured. Realizing that as a female I was an obvious target for comment, I had taken great pains not to ask for anything that could possibly be construed as a special favor. Like the rest of the correspondents, when not sleeping on the ground at the front with an individual unit, I usually occupied a table top in the big, sprawling room at Taejon from which we telephoned. The custom was to come back from the front, bang out your story, and stretch out on the table top. You would try to sleep, despite the noise of other stories being shouted into the phone, till your turn came to read your story to Tokyo. Then, no matter what the hour, you would probably start out again because the front lines were changing so fast you could not risk staying away any longer than necessary.

General Walton H. Walker had ousted Maggie because she was a female and "there are no facilities for ladies at the front." Maggie retorted that there was no lack of bushes in Korea. She appealed Walker's declaration all the way to MacArthur at headquarters and stayed on the job until she was forced to take a train from the battle zone to army headquarters. When she arrived, hoping to make a personal plea to Walker, she was greeted by an army captain who put her in a jeep. The captain, armed with a carbine and a pair of armed soldiers, escorted Maggie directly to the airstrip. As they sped along, the captain "further clarified his views on women correspondents."

By the time Maggie landed in Tokyo, MacArthur had rescinded the order to expel her from Korea. None other than Helen Rogers Reid, president of the *New York Herald Tribune* had cabled MacArthur—whose word was law in that part of the world—asking him to permit Maggie to go back to work. MacArthur's orders read: "Ban on women in Korea being lifted. Marguerite Higgins held in highest professional esteem by everyone."

Back to work Maggie went. She was eating breakfast at US Army headquarters at Chingdoi, situated in an old wooden schoolhouse, when bullets and grenades blew through the walls.

I started to say something to Martin [Harold Martin of the *Saturday Evening Post*] as he crouched by the telephone methodically recording the battle in his notebook. My teeth were chattering uncontrollably, I discovered, and in shame I broke off after the first disgraceful squeak of words.

Certain that her life was ending, Maggie felt surprised that death was going to happen to her.

Then, as the conviction grew, I became hard inside and comparatively calm. I ceased worrying. Physically the result was that my teeth stopped chattering and my hands ceased shaking. This was a relief, as I would have been acutely embarrassed had any one caught me in that state.

Fortunately, by the time [Colonel John] Michaelis came around the corner and said, "How you doin', kid?" I was able to answer in a respectably self-contained tone of voice, "Just fine, sir."

When the fighting grew desperate and casualties overwhelmed army medics, Maggie picked up glass bottles of blood plasma to administer to wounded soldiers. The grateful commander wrote a letter to the *Herald Tribune* extolling Maggie's bravery under fire. From then on, Maggie carried a carbine (rifle) when she rode shotgun in Keyes Beech's jeep. It would not have done any damage against a Soviet tank, but the carbine represented some kind of defense against North Korean soldiers.

By early August 1950, the North Koreans had pushed so far south that UN forces were squeezed into a small area of southeast South Korea. All the Americans could do was defend themselves until more soldiers, supplies, and aircraft could arrive to rejuvenate them. On September 15, MacArthur struck back at North Korea by staging an amphibious assault on the peninsula's west coast at Inchon, 30 miles from Seoul.

Marguerite Higgins typing in an army office in Korea, her face dirty from working in the field. *Marguerite Higgins Collection, Special Collections Research Center, Syracuse University Library*

Maggie needed to get to the scene by ship, but the US Navy forbade access because she was a woman. Just as fast, her luck changed when there was a mix-up in paperwork. Maggie found herself allowed to board the USS *Henrico*, the command ship of a group of transports. She was at sea four days until it was time to drop into a landing craft and go ashore. Her memoir left a blunt, picturesque review of how a fighting man carried out an assault from the sea:

> At three o'clock orders went out to lower the rectangular, flat-bottomed craft into the sea, and the squeaks of turning winches filled the air. From the deck I watched the same operation on the other transports, strung out down the channel as far as the eye could travel.

I was to go in the fifth wave to hit Red Beach. In our craft would be a mortar outfit, some riflemen, a photographer, John Davies of the Newark *Daily News*, and Lionel Crane of the London *Daily Express*.

There was a final briefing emphasizing the split-second timing that was so vital. The tide would be at the right height for only four hours. We would strike at 5:30, half an hour before dead high. Assault waves, consisting of six landing craft lined up abreast, would hit the beach at two-minute intervals. This part of the operation had to be completed within an hour in order to permit the approach of larger landing ship tanks (LSTs), which would supply us with all our heavy equipment. The LSTs would hit the beach at high tide and then, as the waters ebbed away, be stranded helplessly on the mud flats. After eight o'clock, sea approaches to the assaulting marines would be cut off until the next high tide. It was a risk that had to be taken.

Maggie worked her way down the ship's side, hanging onto a net as she felt with her feet for the swaying rungs underneath. She "dropped last into the boat, which was now packed with 38 heavily laden marines, ponchos on their backs and rifles on their shoulders" as they waited for the rest of the landing craft in wave number five. Some of the marines were playing cards.

Finally we pulled out of the circle and started toward the assault control ship, nine miles down the channel. . . .

Red Beach stretched out flatly directly behind the sea wall. Then after several hundred yards it rose sharply to form a cliff on the left side of the beach. Behind the cliff was a cemetery, one of our principal objectives.

At the control ship we circled again, waiting for H hour.

Aircraft carriers and navy cruisers bombarded the beach in a final pounding. There was silence, until an air assault swept over the landing craft. Silence again followed, and then another assault. Then more silence.

The control ship signaled that it was our turn. "Here we go keep your heads down!" shouted Lieutenant [R. J.] Shening. As we rushed toward the sea wall an amber-colored star shell burst above the beach. It meant that our first objective, the cemetery, had been taken. But before we could even begin to relax, brightly colored tracer bullets cut across our bow and across the open top of our boat. I heard the authoritative rattle of machine guns. Somehow the enemy had survived the terrible pounding they'd been getting. No matter what had happened to the first four waves, the Reds had sighted us and their aim was excellent. We all hunched deep into the boat.

"Look at their faces now," John Davies whispered to me. The faces of the men in our boat, including the gin-rummy players, were contorted with fear.

Their boat smashed into the sea wall as bullets whined overhead. The marines still crouched in the boat.

"Come on, you big, brave marines let's get the hell out of here," yelled Lieutenant Shening, emphasizing his words with good, hard shoves.

The first marines were now clambering out of the bow of the boat. The photographer announced that he had had enough and was going straight back to the transport with the boat. For a second I was tempted to go with him. Then a new burst of fire made me decide to get out of the boat fast. I maneuvered my typewriter into a position where I could reach it once I had dropped over the side. I got a footing on the steel ledge on the side of the boat and pushed myself over. I landed in about three feet of water in the dip of the sea wall.

A warning burst, probably a grenade, forced us all down, and we snaked along on our stomachs over the boulders to a sort of curve below the top of the dip. It gave us a cover of sorts from the tracer bullets, and we three newsmen and most of the marines flattened out and waited there. . . .

One marine ventured over the ridge, but he jumped back so hurriedly that he stamped one foot hard onto my bottom. This fortunately has considerable padding, but it did hurt, and I'm afraid I said somewhat snappishly, "Hey, it isn't as frantic as all that." He removed his foot hastily and apologized in a tone that indicated his amazement that he had been walking on a woman. . . .

Suddenly there was a great surge of water. A huge LST was bearing down on us, its plank door halfway down. A few more feet and we would be smashed. Everyone started shouting and, tracer bullets or not we got out of there."

Maggie's typewriter survived the assault, but she never explained how she kept her paper dry.

Maggie made it to the navy's flagship USS *Mount McKinley*, the only place any reporter could file a story about the invasion of Inchon. Then she was discovered and forbidden to return to the *McKinley* between 9 PM and 9 AM, a distinct disadvantage because *New York Times* reporters could file a story when she couldn't. She slept on shore, greatly annoyed that the male reporters who bunked on the *McKinley* had real eggs, not the disgusting powdered kind, for breakfast.

After the Korean War, Marguerite Higgins married General Bill Hall in 1952. They had three children. Their first arrived premature and lived only five days. Maggie's heart was broken. She had seen death so many times, and she had thought about soldiers' families who would grieve when an army chaplain knocked on their doors. Following her daughter's death, she was grateful for "the warmth and new life infused in me by the compassion of others," she wrote in *News is a Singular Thing*, her memoir published in 1955. It was the first time that Maggie admitted that she understood what real compassion was.

Just in her mid-30s when she sat down to reflect on the 11 years she'd worked as a war correspondent, Maggie's words spoke with a growing maturity and self-awareness about the story of her own life.

> For the simplest facts—the difficulty of love, the futility of resentment, man's degradation under tyranny—do not really come through to me until I find them out myself from personal experience . . . until I made these journeys they meant nothing, for I did not understand how they applied to me and to my times.

It was unusual in the 1950s for a married woman with children to work outside her home. Maggie Higgins did—and she kept her own name on her byline. She traveled back and forth to war zones through the rest of that decade and went to Vietnam 10 times, starting in 1963. That year she won prestige by becoming a columnist for *Newsday*.

Sometime during her travels to Southeast Asia, she was bitten by a sand flea that infected her with a fatal illness. Doctors couldn't determine what she had for weeks until they diagnosed leishmaniasis, a flesh-eating tropical disease, but they had no effective way to treat her. (Leishmaniasis is treated today with a round of antibiotics costing less than $10.) As she grew more ill, she was moved to Walter Reed Army Hospital, where Maggie continued to work in her hospital bed.

On January 3, 1966, she died at Walter Reed; she was buried in Arlington National Cemetery. Marguerite Higgins Hall was 45 and left two young children and her husband.

In the later part of the 1900s, Marguerite Higgins became the subject of both popular biographies and scholarly research in women's history that raised questions. Was Marguerite Higgins the cold, scheming, take-no-prisoners woman portrayed by some of her biographers? Or was Higgins condemned because she was a woman who behaved like a man in going after what she wanted?

In his memoir, *Tokyo and Points East*, Keyes Beech devoted a chapter to Maggie Higgins. Beech, who liked and respected women, drew an evenhanded assessment of his coworker. Yet in the same passage, Beech's words reflected a view of women common to men of his generation:

Despite her success, Higgins never gave her readers what they really wanted. What they wanted was the "woman's angle" on war. To her credit, Higgins never stooped to that. Any one of her dispatches might have been written by a man.

In her quest for fame, Higgins was appallingly single-minded. Almost frightening in her determination to overcome all obstacles. But so far as her trade was concerned, she had more guts, more staying power, and more resourcefulness than 90 percent of her detractors. She was a good newspaperman.

It was a tragedy for the world to lose Marguerite Higgins at such a young age. No doubt there was much more for her to say.

5

Ancient Peoples, Modern Wars 1955–1985

In 1956, a junior senator from Massachusetts, John F. Kennedy, declared that "South Vietnam represents the cornerstone of the Free World in Southeast Asia." South Vietnam's strategic location along the east coast of Indochina made it the perfect spot for the US military to take a stand for democracy against North Vietnam, whose Communist government and Viet Minh soldiers had struggled for independence as far back as World War II. The weak, corrupt South Vietnamese government had its own internal enemies: the Vietcong, Communist guerillas who were backed by North Vietnam.

Senator Kennedy became President Kennedy in 1961, and his administration stood determined to combat Communism in small but strategic countries such as Cuba, just 90 miles from the Florida coast, and Vietnam, thousands of miles away but equally vital in the Cold War confrontation against the Soviet Union and Communist China. The Kennedy administration sent military advisors to South Vietnam in 1961, and President Lyndon Johnson, who succeeded Kennedy after his assassination in 1963, approved a massive transfer of US military equipment and combat soldiers to safeguard South Vietnam, beginning in 1965.

From the air, American B-52 strategic bombers attacked North Vietnam and dropped bombs along the Ho Chi Minh Trail, its supply line to the south. On the ground, US infantrymen fought a guerilla war in Vietnam's jungles and highlands. By 1968 there were more than 500,000 American troops in Vietnam.

The war was a disaster for all involved. One million Vietnamese people, civilians and military, died from 1965 to 1975, and

Combat photojournalist Dickey Chapelle (born Georgette Meyer in 1919) covered World War II, Korea, and Vietnam. On November 4, 1965, as she patrolled with US Marines near a South Vietnamese river, the Marine just ahead tripped a Vietcong land mine. He survived, but shrapnel tore open her throat. Dickey Chapelle died minutes later. AP photographer Henri Huet recorded these last moments as an Army chaplain gave her the last rites of the Roman Catholic Church.
©*Associated Press*

the United States lost 58,220 soldiers, sailors, airmen, and nurses. The United States became a nation divided by the conflict. Bitter arguments about the country's role in Vietnam divided Americans into "hawks," supporters for the war effort, and "doves," those who said it was time for the US military to pull out.

The folks at home watched news film shot just the day before on the nation's three television networks: ABC, CBS, and NBC. Black-and-white footage from Vietnam, with reporters on camera to explain the scene, showed disturbing pictures of wounded soldiers and Vietnamese children. Such reporting, plus strong feature reporting in newspapers, brought the war home to Americans as never before.

For the first time, women correspondents were accepted—if not always welcomed—in Vietnam. Martha Gellhorn flew in, as did Marguerite Higgins. There were many others: Liz Trotta of NBC, Denby Fawcett, Ann Bryan Mariano, Beverly Deepe, Kate Webb, Anne Morrissy Merick, Ethel Payne, Jurate Kazickas, Edie Lederer, Tad Bartimus, Tracy Wood, Laura Palmer, and Gloria Emerson.

Gloria Emerson

REPORTING FROM PARIS AND SAIGON

Now Vietnam is our word, meaning an American failure, a shorthand for a disaster, a tragedy of good intentions, a well-meaning misuse of American power, a noble cause ruined by a loss of will and no home front, a war of crime, a loathsome jungle where our army of children fought an army of fanatics.

— Gloria Emerson

It's not typical that someone writes her own obituary. Gloria Emerson did, and friends found it in her apartment after she took her own life on August 4, 2004.

> Gloria Emerson, an award-winning journalist and author who wrote about the war in Vietnam and the Palestinians in Gaza, died at her home in Manhattan at the age of 74. She had been suffering from Parkinson's disease, said her physician Karen Brudney.

Sick with Parkinson's disease, she had lived in pain and despair for the past year. Her doctor—also her friend—knew of her plans and begged her not to follow through. Yet Gloria Emerson, who had watched and written about the pain of others for decades, chose to put an end to hers.

Gloria Emerson was a war reporter for the *New York Times* and covered the Vietnam War in the early 1970s. Her mission was to tell what she saw as truth about the war, the US military presence there, and its impact on ordinary people, both Vietnamese and American. She didn't write the hard news of troop movements, military offensives, bombing runs, or the troubled politics of South Vietnam's shaky, crooked government. Instead, her crisply written profiles drew readers into the experience of vast numbers of Vietnamese caught up in their devastating civil war.

Gloria had listened to people's stories for years. Born in New York City in 1929, she grew up in Manhattan, the daughter of a chorus girl named Ruth Shaw who married an heir, William Emerson, grandson of an oilman who claimed to come from of the same family as the writer-philosopher Ralph Waldo Emerson. Both of Gloria's parents were alcoholics, and her ne'er-do-well father couldn't afford a pricey private school for Gloria, so she attended an all-girl public high school in Manhattan. Gloria wrote poetry for its literary journal, the *Sketchbook*. In a poem, "Rebellion," she voiced a wish to climb to where gulls fly, "And scoop a cloud up in my pocket/And beat my fists against the sky." Gloria wasn't like the other girls. She was sharp-edged and took a no-nonsense approach to life.

When she was a little older, people thought she was an alumna of Vassar College, one of the Seven Sisters colleges. (In Gloria's day, young women were refused entry into all-male Ivy League schools.) The truth was, her father hadn't been able to afford any kind of college for Gloria after she graduated high school in 1946, so she went to work. She got a job with the *New York Journal American*, though she was restricted to writing only for its fashion pages and not under her own name. But for herself, she created an image of polished sophistication. Six feet tall and slender, she was hard to miss at a party. In her 20s, she cut her heavy dark hair in a swingy pageboy and painted her nails dark red, trademark styles she never gave up.

Gloria fell for John "Demi" Gates, a military officer who worked for the Defense Department in a far-off country called Vietnam, a skinny band of land on the Indochina Peninsula in Southeast Asia. Demi's Harvard background and suave demeanor enchanted Gloria, and when he left for the Vietnamese capital of Saigon in 1956, she chased after him. She arrived at Demi's hotel halfway around the world unannounced. He didn't send her home.

Gloria understood that Demi's status as an American military man masked his real job as an intelligence officer. Demi worked for the CIA, one of a pack of "Rover Boys" who quietly circulated through South Vietnam advising its army and carrying out select attacks against Communist interests. Demi had excellent connections, and he found Gloria a job writing public relations pieces for a Filipino relief organization that had quiet links to the CIA.

Early on, Gloria discovered that the best stories came from people doing their jobs. She rode in trucks with Filipino doctors and nurses to care for refugees fleeing the north and Vietnamese peasants who lived in hamlets strung along the Mekong Delta. She sold one piece about the Filipinos to *Reader's Digest* and another to *Mademoiselle* that talked about the brilliant, posh young Americans who lived in Saigon, striving to make South Vietnam a shining example of democracy in Southeast Asia.

Demi returned to the United States in October 1956, ready to leave the CIA and make a fortune in the business world. At that point he and Gloria parted company, because Gloria was far too flamboyant to make a good corporate wife. Besides, she had other plans. Her dry, clever take on fashion and the world at hand had made her friends among other New York fashion writers, and in 1957, her friend Nan Robertson helped find her a job at the *New York Times*. She was also briefly married during this time, though it ended in divorce within a year.

This was the top, what she'd been hoping for, though once again, Gloria was slotted in the women's section in a remote office far from the male staffers who ran the newsroom. In 1957, that's what a girl did—until policy loosened up and some of her coworkers went on to bigger jobs at the *Times*, one as fashion editor, another to the foreign desk and as business editor. (Nan Robertson wrote a book about these newspaperwomen after they sued the *Times* for sex discrimination in 1974 and won, when the case was settled out of court.)

Gloria left her job in 1960 and moved to Belgium where she was married for a year, but like a first marriage in New York, this one also failed. She returned to the *Times* and worked out of its Paris and London offices. Somehow she finagled hard news assignments, especially when the Vietnamese were involved. Through it all she still had the fashion beat; her final *Times* story before she left Europe was the "Lowdown from Paris" about the spring collections of Chanel, Givenchy, and Yves Saint Laurent.

She always campaigned to get to Vietnam, but men who ran the *New York Times* took a dim view of assigning women to cover the war. The prestigious newspaper already had a stable of male war correspondents to call upon. One, an upstart named David Halberstam, had won the Pulitzer Prize in 1964 for his Vietnam reporting.

Then the bosses changed their minds and sent Gloria to Vietnam, "allowed to go," she believed, "because the war was supposed to be over so it didn't matter if a female was sent." In March 1970, when she stepped off the plane and rode to her hotel, she was appalled. Gone was the lovely city that she

Gloria Emerson wrote about ordinary US soldiers during the Vietnam War.
Nancy Moran

remembered from her days as a reporter in 1956, when Saigon's streets were lined with trees and its buildings and shops still bore the mark of French culture. Now Saigon was overrun with American soldiers. Its bar and brothel business thrived, sure of steady business from the Americans who were fighting against the Communist North.

In the coming weeks, Gloria filed stories that ranged wide and ran deep—how war disrupted South Vietnam's middle class, and how the American officials destroyed black market marijuana because soldiers could buy it cheaply—two bucks for a 10-joint pack. She was impressed by Vietnam's 1,000-year history of fighting for independence from any and all outsiders—from China, from France, and now from the United States.

By now Gloria was 40 years old, and her instincts, opinions, and writing were sharper than ever. She caught the small details of war in the field and life in Saigon that other *Times* reporters had missed. Soon after arriving, she spotted a rack of postcards in a Saigon shop that sported scenes from the war that GIs liked to mail home. The bizarre notion of picture postcards with war photos was something that others hadn't picked up on. In her usual two-fingered way, she typed up the story:

EVEN THE POSTCARDS IN SAIGON DEPICT G.I.'S IN BATTLE

SAIGON. SOUTH VIETNAM.
March 6—It is a curious war. There are even colored picture postcards showing scenes of it.

They are sold in the lobbies of some of the expensive hotels and on the sidewalks of the downtown streets, where crowds of Vietnamese stroll and shop on weekends. Not many seem startled by the postcards, which are printed in Hong Kong and have captions such as "Direct hit" or "Mine detecting." There is one called "Night convoy moving cautiously" and another showing three American soldiers investigating a Vietcong trap, with a big arc of barbed wire in the foreground.

The Vietnamese prefer postcards with more sentimental themes and those that cost less money. But some American soldiers on leave in Saigon and the occasional visitor find it fun to send the war postcards home.

They usually show American soldiers in action, but one of Street fighting—one of the few depicting Vietnamese soldiers—has a fairly brisk sale, according to a 14-year-old boy who works in a shop on Le Lol Street. He is not sure why, his own preference being for pictures of large cats or of fat, smiling, white babies. The Americans do not like them.

Gloria Emerson chose her words carefully to convey that bleakness she saw and felt. She was the best kind of writer, one aware that her words, though in print, must ring in readers' minds. Sometimes chunks of her work read like poetry when she repeated a phrase that established a rhythm. To read the opening lines of each paragraph was to grasp the whole story, as in her article about a medevac crew that helicoptered injured soldiers to the hospital, titled "On Med-Evac Copter, Faces and Pain."

"Last Thursday was a typical day for the crew," one paragraph began.

"The first radio call for help was at 8 a.m.," read the next paragraph opener.

"It was the day on which Specialist 5 John H. Parham died . . ."

"I was trying to stop the bleeding, but it was, like, say, hopeless . . ."

"It was the day when 40 South Vietnamese soldiers were mistakenly shot and wounded by an American aircraft . . ."

"It was the day when two Americans, one 21 and one 19, tripped their own anti-personnel mine . . ."

"The younger man had been given morphine . . ."

"The other man was conscious but did not make a sound . . ."

"At the hospital, surgery was performed almost immediately. The younger man's legs were amputated below the knee and the older one's right leg was amputated below the knee . . ."

Gloria interviewed peasants, refugees, captured soldiers, bar girls, and street kids. She wrote about "Sister 5" (of six children), the 11-year-old who sold Christmas cards because making money was more important than going to school. She talked with a Buddhist monk who, hoping to "build a truly sovereign nation, a democratic nation," quietly campaigned against the reelection of South Vietnam's corrupt president, Nguyen Van Thieu. She interviewed imprisoned Vietcong, including women who fought for the Communist North. Once a Vietnamese woman looked at Gloria in her street clothes and ponytail and asked, "What is it?" She'd never seen an American woman.

Gloria also examined the lives of ordinary American GIs, the soldiers and airmen in Vietnam mostly because they'd been drafted. She went on patrol with the "grunts," as soldiers were tagged during the war. She rode with troops in helicopters on their way to the jungle to engage the enemy, and she returned in UH-1 "Huey" utility choppers loaded with gravely injured young men. She watched one 20-year-old chopper pilot fly while keeping an eye on his precious, wounded cargo and talked with a broken-hearted medic whose best friend had been killed a week earlier.

There were others, the GIs who sported peace symbols and "FTA" ("fuck the army") on their helmets, and those who used heroin openly in front of their officers. Some hated Asians, calling them by the racist term "gooks." Another, a bitter 20-year-old communications specialist, bore a "warrior sense of revenge" for his six buddies killed in "'Nam.'" All had stories to tell, and Gloria Emerson made it her job to get those stories out.

The United States had begun drawing down the number of troops in Vietnam a year earlier, a massive figure that had swelled to 543,000. The fighting seemed endless, and to many, pointless, but there was plenty of action for a war-weary military. In 1970, when Gloria got to Vietnam, the press was war-weary as well. Every afternoon, as they had for five years, newsmen and the handful of women reporters working out of Saigon gathered for the "Five O'Clock Follies," the military's daily briefing. Few believed that the press conference was anything more than a joke without any kind of credibility. Frequently they tossed barbs and made fun of the hapless information officers tasked with the briefings. Highly skeptical that the army was going to say anything useful or unembellished, veteran reporters preferred to gather news themselves. They depended on their own sources to get the story straight.

In July 1970, Gloria's *Times* article revealed that the South Vietnamese government crammed political prisoners—editors, students, and the like—into cramped "tiger cages" made of stone on the prison island of Con Son. Newsmen were refused entry, so Gloria got her story from a church worker who accompanied two US congressmen on a fact-finding tour of Vietnam. The news caused an uproar, embarrassed President Thieu, and added to antiwar sentiments in the United States. A few days later, Gloria interviewed one of the prisoners—he'd been released, but his legs had withered to the point that he could not walk. Even later, she reported the news when the Thieu government expelled the man who had revealed the tiger cages in the first place.

Late that October, Gloria broke the news that an American general had received the army's Silver Star, a top honor, based on a made-up story. Her lead, the opening paragraph to a damning report, gave the truth straight up:

> FACTS INVENTED FOR A GENERAL'S MEDAL
> By Gloria Emerson
> Special to the *New York Times*
>
> SAIGON, SOUTH VIETNAM, OCT. 20—The United States Army has awarded a Silver Star for valor to a general in Vietnam based on a description of acts of heroism in Cambodia that were invented by enlisted men under orders.
>
> The decoration was presented last Thursday to Brigadier General Eugene P. Forrester, who was then assistant division commander. . . .
>
> An Army spokesman has said that General Forrester had not seen the citation and that the general did not know that enlisted men had used more imagination than facts to write it.

In December, Gloria journeyed to Nnhokat Ridge near the DMZ—the demilitarized zone between North and South Vietnam—to interview brand-new American soldiers who had been drafted into the army. Their armored vehicle had run over a mine, and now the raw newcomers had a superstition:

> TO COMPANY B, APRICOTS SUGGEST DEATH.

Private Hobbs has stopped eating the apricots in the C-rations because he wants to stay alive and unhurt. Most of the other enlisted men in his squad do the same. Nor will they let anyone who has eaten apricots ride on their vehicle.

"The day we hit the mine, a sergeant ate apricots," Private Hobbs related. "If a guy eats apricots, he's not coming with us." . . .

Because the men rarely see the enemy, a feeling of hopelessness has grown in the company. The ground is old ground, covered by other Americans in the same huge, heavy machines years ago, when some of the current crop were boys in school.

"It seems so futile—these guys are not even fighting for a cause," Specialist 4 Edmund Burke, a medic, said. "And I've only seen three dinks in six months." "Dink" is slang for the enemy.

He remembers Nov. 12, when Private Hobbs's vehicle hit the mine.

"There was a sergeant in the hatch, his face all messed up," the medic said, "and when I got to him he was saying over and over, 'I've lost all my teeth, I've lost all my teeth.'"

Gloria Emerson's reporting outraged the army's top brass and jangled nerves in Washington. The vocabulary she chose, words such as "futility," "helplessness," "boredom," "apathy," and "bitterness," appearing as they did in a single *New York Times* article, helped convince many Americans that it was time to bring their soldiers home from Vietnam. Others blamed reporters like Emerson for adding to the problems the war had created. Angry hawks, backers of America's military mission to Vietnam, accused her and other journalists of undercutting morale among soldiers and airmen.

The following February, the *New York Times* reported that Gloria was named a George Polk Award winner for her articles reporting on how the war had affected individuals in Vietnam.

Gloria Emerson was as sharp as her words. Her colleagues thought she was ferocious, fearless, and generous as well. She welcomed young reporters to Vietnam and gave them advice whether they wanted it or not. On a Saigon street in 1970, she flagged down a young woman named Judith Coburn and took her by the arm:

> She [Gloria] jerked me by the arm and brought me into a coffee shop, and she said, "Sit down," which I did. She said, "*Village Voice*, you're here from the *Village Voice*." And I said yes. She said, "I'm Gloria Emerson. . . . So," she said, "no one is going to tell you how it works here." And she ordered some ice tea and began talking about her experiences.
>
> I remember dodging the ice tea, because she was gesturing with her spoon and gobs of ice tea were coming out. Finally, I actually managed to get a question into the conversation, and I said, "Well, so what's it like out there? The war, covering combat." I sort of knew you weren't supposed to ask anybody this directly, but I thought maybe Gloria would tell me. She looked at me and said, "Judith, there is only one thing you have to know about combat. When you get out there, all you are going to have to know, is where you are going to have to go to the bathroom." I didn't say anything. She said . . . "The story is what is happening to the Vietnamese. Don't get into that bang-bang stuff, that's what the boys are doing."

Gloria returned from Vietnam and kept reporting for the *Times* until the mid-1970s. She wrote a book about her personal past in Vietnam, *Winners & Losers*. She taught seminars at Princeton University and creative writing to Vietnam vets in Boston. She was known for her generosity to street people. When others asked Gloria to reflect on her own Vietnam experiences, she refused, replying to one request that Vietnam was "such a dark and powerful and terrible thing in my life." She said that outsiders couldn't understand those years in Vietnam, its tragedies and its grief.

Gloria had no patience for grandstanding or other people's pet causes that couldn't compare with the atrocities of life in Vietnam. Unlike many Americans who took out their antiwar views on returning Vietnam veterans by humiliating them or ignoring their problems returning to normal lives, she sympathized with the young men who came home jobless, drug-addicted, or mentally unstable. She took on rock star John Lennon and his wife Yoko Ono when they staged a "Bed-In for Peace" against the Vietnam War in 1969, famously calling out Lennon for being ridiculous and naive if he thought he'd saved a single life.

Gloria also disparaged America's second wave of feminists, the angry protesters who took to American streets in the 1970s. She had met women in Vietnam who had lost their husbands, children, homes, and way of life, women whose lives were truly desperate. By comparison, Gloria observed, American women had little to complain about. "I could not rejoice [at feminism] when women I knew went back to school to be lawyers or doctors," she said later, "when in 1973 I knew 11 Vietnam veterans without college degrees."

In 1989 Gloria flew to Israel to cover her "second war," as she thought of it. She lived among Palestinians who lived in homes and camps along the Gaza Strip, where an *intifada* (uprising) against Israel had started in 1987. She was a crusader for the Palestinians and openly declared that Israel oppressed them. She called for a Palestinian homeland, an extremely unpopular view among most Americans, who thought of Palestinians as terrorists, following suicide bombings, hijackings of airliners and cruise ships in the 1970s and '80s, and attacks on Israeli athletes and US Marines. Famously private, Gloria Emerson refused most requests for interviews in her later years. Joyce Hoffmann, author of *On Their Own: Women Journalists and the American Experience in Vietnam*, asked for an interview and was turned down. Gloria changed her mind sometime later, when she agreed to write the introduction for a collection of memoirs of other women who had worked and reported in Vietnam during the war.

Gloria Emerson never forgot Vietnam. She was in her late 70s when the United States and its allies invaded Iraq in 2003 to overthrow the government of Saddam Hussein. Outraged, Gloria vented to her friend Rod Nordland, a younger reporter who was covering Iraq for *Newsweek* magazine. At her memorial service, Nordland spoke about his friend and how her experience in Vietnam had stayed with her:

> "It's absolutely disgusting, isn't it?" she'd say. "There's no hope at all. It'll be just as bad as that [Vietnam] was, I can't bear to think of it." Yet she did, a great deal; she followed [the Iraq War] religiously, she watched every major network and most of the cable news programs on it, read everything we wrote about it, even had computer-using friends print out Web stories on it for her. It wasn't her war the way Vietnam was, of course. The last time I saw her, in July, she said, with some regret, "I'll never be able to go there." . . . . Whenever I saw her she'd pepper me with questions about Iraq, and then browbeat me, saying, "You mustn't keep going there," and then finally she'd add, "but of course you have to, dear," and just as abruptly she'd change the subject. I think that Iraq and this sense of here we go again, just made her sad.

Georgie Anne Geyer

REPORTING FROM HAVANA, GUATEMALA CITY, TBILISI, AND BAGHDAD

Being from the South Side of Chicago, where life was real, the romance of "revolution" and "liberation" never captured me.

—Georgie Anne Geyer

In November 1980, a veteran American reporter flew from Chicago to Amman, Jordan, so she could hail a taxi. There was no direct flight from the United States to Baghdad, Iraq, her final destination. But in Amman, Jordan's capital city, Arabs were friendly enough to American journalists, and she hired her taxi with no problem. Accompanied by two male reporters from other newspapers, she sped east 750 miles across the desert to Baghdad. Her name was Georgie Anne Geyer, and her plan was to interview Iraq's minister of information, Tariq Aziz, the mouthpiece for Iraq's dictator Saddam Hussein.

The United States had no diplomatic ties with either Baghdad or Tehran, Iran, but foreign correspondents such as Georgie Anne Geyer—Gee Gee to her friends—could go places and ask questions where American officials couldn't. Iraq and its bigger neighbor Iran were at war, both Muslim nations yet sworn enemies divided by culture and religion.

Gee Gee had questions for Aziz, especially about why Iraq had launched an invasion across the desert into Iran. Did Iraq plan to seize Iran's vast oil fields? Was Saddam Hussein, a Sunni Muslim, hoping to kill Iran's Shiite religious dictator, the Ayatollah Khomeini? And what was Saddam's thinking on the ever-present troubles between Jews and Arabs in Israel? Gee Gee had scored an interview with Saddam seven years earlier, and now she hoped for the best: to come face-to-face with his spokesman, Tariq Aziz, an elegant, English-speaking Iraqi Christian who steered his way through his talk with her as carefully as he steered his way as a member of Saddam's Revolutionary Command Council.

When she was finally escorted into Aziz's office after a 12-day wait in Baghdad—all her careful planning had never landed her an actual appointment at the Ministry of Information—Gee Gee was direct with Aziz. Why had Iraq invaded Iran? "For one reason only," he said. "Because Khomeini was trying to put the entire region in flames, to destroy the borders and reignite the struggles of the sixth and seventh centuries, when Islam swept from Arabia to Spain."

Gee Gee had read wide and deep about the Middle East and its intriguing, violent past, which seemed so strange to most Americans. Now at the age of 45, she felt at ease interpreting this sweep of history for readers of her thrice-weekly newspaper column. She was comfortable in her own skin. The hesitation, shyness, and guilt that might have plagued her in her 20s were gone. After all these years she "simply knew things."

Gee Gee Geyer was out to know the truth, to discover what made people tick. As a girl growing up on Chicago's South Side, she had watched people up close and personal. Life was like that for kids who lived with their families in tidy bungalows in her neighborhood, folks trying to keep food on the table as the United States lived through the Great Depression. Gee Gee's father was a dairyman. Robert George Geyer, a giant, ham-fisted man of German ancestry, lived out his principles of honesty, self-reliance, and hard work. He refused to have anything to do with Chicago's political machine and its crooked building inspectors, who sent Mafia men to collect $5,000 and $10,000 bribes and were perfectly willing to see small dairies like Geyer's swallowed up by big ones. "If you were not Irish or one of the machine ethnic groups, you weren't in—especially Germans, with their individualistic tendencies toward their own businesses," Gee Gee wrote about her dad. As a youth, he had steered clear of a gang of Irish toughs on the streets, including a boy named Richard Daley, who grew up to become Chicago's mayor and political boss of the city's Democratic machine.

Gee Gee Geyer inherited her father's hatred of bullies, never to become, as she said, "one of those suburban relativists, bred in suburbia where liberalism was easy." On the city's tribal streets she knew there was "a very real bully on every block." There were other reasons to feel uneasy on the streets of Chicago; most of Gee Gee's white neighbors feared or hated Chicago's black residents, who lived in their own parts of town. Sometimes Gee Gee broke the rules and ventured into the city's black neighborhoods to sit and talk with the old men on their front stoops when the weather was good.

Gee Gee was an intense young girl. She *needed* to learn about these old men and about so much more in life. She asked serious questions about human existence, questions that many adults never considered. She lay awake at night wondering about her own place on earth. "What if one person in the world knew the truth," she asked herself, "and that person was a woman and she could not speak?"

Her mother, Georgie Hazel Geyer, taught Gee Gee how to write and to dream of travel to faraway lands, even as she complained about her own load of housework. Though Gee Gee's mother clearly felt stuck in her role as a homemaker, she expected Gee Gee to grow up, marry, and become a housewife too. Decades later, Gee Gee wrote, "My choosing a profession,

I am sure, struck her as a betrayal until later in life, when she came to understand and even prize it."

It was Gee Gee's brother Glen, 10 years her senior, who became another source of strength in her life. Glen, like his mother, had a creative soul and grew up to be a well-respected dress designer in Chicago. He played with his little sister, creating for her a charming fantasy world that fed her imagination, and he encouraged her to become a journalist when she grew up.

"My family simply told me in every way that the world was open to me," Gee Gee Geyer wrote when she looked back on her long career. In the fall of 1952 she entered the Medill School of Journalism at Northwestern University. There she learned the ins and outs of becoming a *reporter*—not a media specialist or journalist as such men and women called themselves in later times—but a *reporter* trained to learn the facts of a story and write it well. She adored history, political science, and literature, and she despised the hands-on classes that Medill required.

I particularly resented typesetting. There I was a senior ready to go out in the world and wanting to be prepared for it by knowing everything—history, philosophy, physics . . . things that might lead a seeking person to knowledge and wisdom. And *we* seniors, at the height of our searching, were standing two full afternoons a week, setting type *by hand*.

No matter that newspapers no longer set type that way. No matter that they were wasting our time with woebegone formalities. That was required.

Gee Gee didn't embark on a career in reporting when she graduated. She won a highly prized Fulbright Scholar Award, and in 1956 she headed to Vienna, Austria. In October, she awoke to the news that neighboring Hungarians had revolted against their Soviet occupiers, and refugees poured across the border into Austria. The uprising was short-lived. The Russians crushed the revolution, imprisoning thousands of Hungarians who had demanded their freedom from Communism.

With a busload of students, Gee Gee rode to the border, her first time as an eyewitness to true human suffering. She served food to stricken refugees who had nothing but their freedom. Heartbroken, Gee Gee asked herself how such things could happen. "Heroism had failed. Goodness had lost. What was the matter with the world?"

Then the world turned on her. When Gee Gee returned home the next fall, she was desperately sick with hepatitis. She spent an entire year in bed, two months of that in a coma, and marked her slow recovery by how high she could raise her hands over her head. It was a tough lesson for a young woman who had felt invincible, and it taught Gee Gee the value of patience, that sometimes she would have to play the waiting game.

After she recovered, Gee Gee followed the same path that other Medill graduates took and went to work for a small newspaper. In 1960, she landed her dream job at the *Chicago Daily News*. Every day she watched the reporters who milled around the city desk, hard-driving, crusty men—and the two lone women permitted to work with them. They were newspapermen (even the women), a solid team hard at work competing with the other three dailies in the big newspaper town of Chicago.

The *Daily News* was also a paper quite unlike papers today; it was journalism quite unlike journalism today. We quite simply "reported" what was going on. We did not write columns or our own personal interpretations on the news pages. We reported fires and murders and investigations and the statements of institutions. It was a much straighter and much more honest job then, and it was also a hell of a lot of fun.

Gee Gee Geyer got her first big story at the *Daily News* by dressing up as a cocktail waitress and listening in on conversations as she served champagne at a Mafia wedding in Chicago. The next Monday, her story and photo appeared on the front page with the lead "The mob went to a party and I went along for the ride." But for the most part, her days were filled with less risky stuff, the nuts and bolts of reporting crime, fires, city politics, and school news.

She got to know neighborhood organizers, including a reputed radical named Saul Alinsky, who, the conservative Gee Gee felt, was unfairly labeled a dangerous man. She admired Alinsky's dedication to improving life for Chicago's underprivileged people, and his honesty too. (Alinsky had famously refused a bribe from "Hizzoner" Mayor Daley.) She studied his tactics and learned from them. When City Hall threatened to tear down Jane Addams' aging settlement building, Hull-House, a Chicago and American landmark, Gee Gee organized a group to save it and won.

Still, Georgie Anne Geyer longed for an overseas assignment. *Daily News* foreign correspondents were all men in their 50s and 60s, so there seemed to be no chance of her getting out of Chicago. Then in 1964, she got her break when she won a grant to study in Latin America and her editor agreed to let her report from there for the paper. After all, she was traveling on someone else's tab.

Gee Gee flew to Peru and set out to write a feature on a sister city project between Pensacola, Florida, and Chimbote, a seaside city. Kids in Pensacola were raising money for Chimbote to build a sports stadium, a gift for Chimbote's impoverished children. On the surface, everything looked good, until some local newspapermen hinted at dirty dealings. In the classic tradition of reporters, Gee Gee asked around and discovered the donor of land for the new project was the biggest crook in town. He owned a brothel across the street.

Gee Gee requested an interview, and he agreed but was careful not to show his hand as they talked. It took a long hot afternoon and many glasses of red wine before Gee Gee, feeling desperate for information, decided to appeal to the man's vanity. "I see that you are an intelligent man . . . a man as smart as you would not give up something without getting some for himself." Indeed not. The egotistical crook brought out blueprints. One glance, and Gee Gee made out a ring of small rooms inside the stadium. They were meant for a new brothel.

"The bishop of Chimbote waxed ashen when he got the story—then he was enraged," Gee Gee recalled. Pensacola quietly dropped its sister city project.

Gee Gee made her first trip to a war zone when civil war erupted in the Dominican Republic. Early on, her editor argued that a street war was no place for a woman and offered to send her to Vietnam, where she'd be safe in a Saigon hotel. This was a ludicrous suggestion, and when she gave him an I-cannot-believe-you-just-said-that look, he agreed to let her go to Santo Domingo. But her editor's worries stuck with her, and Gee Gee felt sick with panic as she packed for the trip, convinced she'd get shot the moment she arrived.

When the plane's door opened and Gee Gee looked out at dozens of Marines at the Santo Domingo airport, some of them shirtless in the Caribbean heat, she relaxed—and realized that she was learning a life lesson. "In that languid scene," she wrote when she looked back later, "I lost forever that kind of inordinate, unspecified, undifferentiated fear. There were times when I was afraid later, but never like that."

Gee Gee happily found herself living the reporter's dream. In the Hotel Embajador were newsmen, diplomats, generals, exiled leaders from neighboring Haiti, writers, and curiosity seekers. There was a 7 PM curfew, so in the hotel bar "every night we argued, drank, brawled, and fought the Battle of Santo Domingo." Emotions ran hot in bitter arguments between the "democrats," Juan Bosch supporters, and conservatives who backed old members of the Rafael Trujillo dictatorship because they opposed communism. Gee Gee believed that Bosch was a constitutionally elected president and that President Lyndon Johnson had made a mistake sending in the Marines to back the other side. It was not the first time she would discover that the US government didn't have a clear understanding of Latin American politics.

Reporters had access to the warring parties, and Gee Gee adored that. "We—and only we—could go to all sides. Only we could know everything. Only we could put all the pieces of a complicated puzzle together." As she carried out her interviews, she began to realize something more: she must report not just whats but whys. The Dominican Republic had its own history and culture that she must understand and interpret for her American readers.

She asked around about the talented but troubled young rebels, "fanatics" she thought, who were fighting for the revolution. Why would they fight to the death? A local professor gave her the answer. "What you have here is the problem of desperation," he explained. "They have a suicidal feeling that is aroused by conflict with a great power. You have a small person, who's proud, and he feels that he has nothing to lose but his life, so 'Go ahead and kill me.'"

It was a pathology—a pattern, Gee Gee discovered—that she witnessed among rebels and terrorists time and again over the next 50 years. Desperate young men were willing—even hoped—to die fighting Americans and others in places such as the Dominican Republic, Vietnam, Guatemala, Nicaragua, El Salvador, Iraq, and Afghanistan. It was a pattern that continued to puzzle Americans and the US government.

In the spring of 1966 Gee Gee turned her eyes to Cuba, hoping to get an interview with Fidel Castro. No one had seen the young dictator for months, and rumors flew that Castro was sick or dead. Several times Gee Gee missed her chance to leave from Santo Domingo for Cuba, and there weren't any flights from the United States. Still in Santo Domingo, she was sure Castro's people had her request, but she was a long time waiting for a reply. She ended up going home to Chicago to visit her sick father, and then the call came. With no direct flights from the US to Communist Cuba, Gee Gee arrived in Havana via Mexico City. There, without warning, she was whisked away to see the ghostly Castro.

Gee Gee was empty handed, without pen or notebooks. Castro began a long-winded meeting, and all Gee Gee could rely on were her ears and her memory.

I could take no chance on losing this apparition, so I began to work out a certain method I later perfected. I learned to focus—virtually to set my mind on—certain important phrases as he uttered them. I had the conscious feeling of a hand coming out of my mind and grasping them and freezing them for a moment. I found that with this method I could keep quotes perfectly for at least three days.

Before the days of digital images, Georgie Anne Geyer stashed snapshots of her newspaper clips in scrapbooks. *Courtesy of Georgie Anne Geyer*

Gee Gee found Castro captivating—both sweet and ruthless—an ego-bound man who was motivated not by money or women but pure power. Castro *was* the revolution, the idol of agitated young rebels around the globe. He talked endlessly, carrying on a seven-hour interview with Gee Gee that was interrupted only when Castro decided to go out for ice cream. He made a point of boasting that Cubans had 28 flavors, more than the Howard Johnson's chain in the United States. (After Gee Gee's interview with Castro ran in American papers, Howard Johnson's stated it now had 32.) The *Chicago Daily News* proudly ran a photo of Gee Gee and Castro under the astonishing headline: OUR MAN IN HAVANA IS A GIRL.

Again Gee Gee felt frustrated that she couldn't fully understand Cuba and its revolution. How, she asked, could Cubans flip from their lives as Westerners in a Christian nation to Communism and its official atheism? But over the next two months in Cuba, when she was Castro's guest many times, she realized that a cult of personality surrounded Castro. For many, the Cuban dictator fit the Latin American notion of a *caudillo*—a charismatic strongman. Castro exerted "mind control," she wrote.

In 1968 the *Daily News* sent Gee Gee to another revolution, this time in the jungle mountains of Guatemala. She wanted to interview rebel guerillas, well-educated young Marxists who hid from the authorities as they tried to bring about a people's revolution among Guatemala's wretchedly poor peasants. Gee Gee knew there was no point in asking for a meeting directly, because no one would acknowledge it. One simply didn't talk about these things openly. "You're not playing games; you're playing with temperaments turned to calculated and sometimes spontaneous brutality, all revolutionary collegiality one moment and calculated savagery the next." Again she played the waiting game by "looking around" Guatemala City, hoping to make things happen.

Her patience paid off. On a tip, she paid a social call to a lawyer who belonged to the Communist Party, and before she left, hinted that she'd like to meet the guerillas. "But you know I have nothing whatsoever to do with them," he replied smoothly. "Oh, I know, I know that," Gee Gee assured him. But the polite stranger was well connected, and Gee Gee got her meeting with the guerrillas after a "dramatic ballet" of a car ride to their hideout. She wrote up the story, tucked it in her purse, went to a cocktail party where she said nothing about the interview, and left Guatemala that night. The *Chicago Daily News* ran her story the next week and syndicated it across the United States.

But she had made enemies. When Gee Gee returned to Guatemala that fall, she was followed. A desk clerk gave her a letter, and she opened it to see a hand outlined on it, the distinctive symbol of Mano Blanca, the White Hand, a right-wing terrorist gang funded by Guatemala's big landowners. The White Hand maimed, mutilated, and killed, not just Marxist rebels but ordinary Guatemalans who wanted to establish a democracy.

We know you are a spy, the letter read, calling Gee Gee a "*puta*," a whore, as well. Gee Gee, who had resented her blond, "Illinois corn-fed" looks, was amused at the irony of it all.

She made contact with the rebels. This time, Gee Gee—clad in sports clothes and ordinary flats—and her photographer, Henry Gill—not in the best shape—trekked far into the mountains to get their interview. They hiked overnight until near daybreak, sleeping on the ground and digging in their feet to keep from rolling off the mountain. Gee Gee spent three days with the rebels and the mix of peasants who fought with them, speaking Spanish and listening to their stories. An old peasant talked of being forced from his village, a story she heard over and over during her years in Central America. A young guerilla startled her by speaking openly and saying that Fidel Castro—the idol of revolutionaries—was a "big egocentric." "But we won't be like that," the rebel promised. Later, Gee Gee would think about his naive promise. "In years to come I would hear that phrase—'We won't be like that; we will be different'—so many, many sad times."

The trek out proved to be dangerous. When the army brushed by, Gee Gee's small party fell flat on the ground. Their guide got them lost, and by the end one big guerilla was pulling Gee Gee up over the rocks as another dragged Henry Gill. In the end, it was worth the effort—the *Daily News* ran a series of articles about the Guatemalan guerillas, and they appeared in newspapers around the world.

Now a "marked woman" in the eyes of the Guatemalan government, Gee Gee took great care whenever she returned. She saw no sign that the White Hand was trailing her, and she began to think she was forgotten. Then in 1972, she returned again. After dinner with a friend, she said good-bye and went to the elevator where she spotted a stranger, "tall, strung-out," who had been in the lobby that afternoon. He missed the elevator, and Gee Gee fled to her room and bolted the door. The elevator doors opened again, and she heard him coming. Her lock turned, but the bolt held fast. She called and a bellman came to the rescue, but by then, her attacker was in the bar and denied everything. Gee Gee knew in her gut that the White Hand had tried to carry out its threat from that long-ago letter.

Through the 1970s and '80s, Gee Gee traveled the troubled world. She reported on Chile's wild ride through an American-style democracy followed by a Marxist government and then a military dictatorship. In Bolivia she investigated the death of the legendary Marxist rebel Ernesto "Che" Guevara. The charismatic Che, second only to Castro in revolutionary glory, had tried to rally Bolivia's indigenous peasants for revolution. After talking with scores of people, including Che's now imprisoned compatriots, Gee Gee concluded that Che had made a giant miscalculation; Bolivia's peasants were nationalists, and many had served in the Bolivian army. Gee Gee talked with people who had known Che on two continents, and she concluded that he was suicidal, that he'd had a death wish, pure and simple. Just the same, she was chilled when a doctor showed her the evidence of his death. The Bolivians had claimed they shot him, but the doctor had kept Che's bloody shirt. He'd been stabbed with a bayonet and a machete; the bullets had followed.

In 1967 Gee Gee went to Moscow when the Cold War was two decades old and hundreds of Soviet nuclear missiles were aimed at American cities. She followed the trail that Peggy Hull, Bessie Beatty, and Rheta Childe Dorr had taken half a century earlier, riding the Trans-Siberian Railway from Vladivostok westward. Along the way she met and interviewed scores of Soviet citizens, from Uzbek farmers to young Muscovites who danced in underground discos. Usually they didn't talk openly. "You learn what is real by pauses and coughs," she wrote. Sometimes a small look or comment encouraged Gee Gee to pry a bit with questions, and an interviewee would spill his or her guts.

Russia was a "torment for any honest journalist." Gee Gee came away convinced that the entire Union of Soviet Socialist Republics, from top to bottom, operated under a code of dishonesty. These people had their souls "hidden deep." In a society where the totalitarian government controlled every part of people's lives from cradle to grave, ordinary men and women couldn't tell the difference between an honest statement and a dishonest one. After all, if the government dictated what was "true," then how could a person know what was real and what was a lie? And how could someone live that way?

It was in Tbilisi, Soviet Georgia, where she nearly died when a television commentator attacked her. Gee Gee always followed a set of her own rules when she traveled alone, living in hotels and dining in restaurants. She was careful not to appear anything but a professional when dealing with strange men in order to stay out of harm's way. Of course, she was hit on from time to time, and Gee Gee noticed that Russian men were especially loutish in their behavior toward women. They didn't even use pick-up lines—they simply lunged.

One day Gee Gee spoke with a well-known television commentator, and after a pleasant interview, she allowed him to buy her an inexpensive dinner. Half an hour later he knocked on her hotel room door, and Gee Gee, thinking it was her female guide, answered it. The TV man, drunk and ugly-faced, attacked her, and when she screamed and fought back, he beat her savagely. He left only after Gee Gee "agreed" to sleep with him when he came to Chicago. By then, she would say anything to get him to stop hitting her.

The next morning, when Gee Gee tried to complain to the authorities, she learned that the newsman had bribed everyone at the hotel to say nothing. She complained to the American embassy, where "her friends" listened to her story and hinted with leering questions that she might have come on to her attacker. When she heard the news, even her own mother said, "Dear, I'm surprised it hasn't happened to you sooner." Gee Gee began to feel shame and asked herself if she actually was guilty, that "good girls" didn't get themselves attacked. And when she came back to Chicago, no one in the office said a word except for the legendary *Daily News* columnist Mike Royko, who observed that if a Russian woman reporter had been beaten up in the US, "it would be around the world in five minutes."

When Gee Gee launched her career as a foreign correspondent in the 1960s, it was unusual for reporters to be targeted. In 2012, after journalist Marie Colvin died in Syria and CBS correspondent Lara Logan was sexually assaulted and nearly killed by a mob in Cairo's Tahrir Square, Gee Gee reflected on how things had changed over 50 years:

> When I went to Latin America, and then to the Middle East, Asia, the Soviet Union, most groups believed in the Geneva Accords, i.e. that journalists were protected noncombatants, like nurses, rescue workers, and people in general who were not armed to fight. Even the Vietcong generally obeyed these rules—the Khmer Rouge in Cambodia did not. That world changed.
>
> Otherwise, I was very careful to dress conservatively, to be respectful of culture, etc. I would, for instance, have worn a hijab or long black robe if I were going into Tahrir Square in Cairo at the height of the revolution there.
>
> But then, I'm not sure that would have really helped, because there you had these Islamic fanatics who would attack any woman. This has completely changed since my days. In 1974 for instance, I went to Saudi Arabia the first time, and I had little problem walking through the markets in a loose dress. Today I am sure that would not be possible.
>
> I would advise young women to cover areas, not events, and to cover them when there is not war or revolution. This way, you get a true sense of the people and you are safer. But—it *is* a different world.

Gee Gee Geyer met "a whole wonderful lineup of men in my life—and of all different types. The Cuban diplomat, the famous Russian leader, the Washington bureau chief, the environmentalist, the Hungarian I worked with at the border during the breakout of 1956 when I was in Vienna, the incredible security agent who worked on the Mafia." She came close to marrying Keyes Beech, the well-regarded veteran reporter at the *Chicago Daily News*; but Gee Gee feared she would lose her personal sovereignty and spirit in a marriage, and she asked herself how she could manage both a career and a family. Her question would become a timeless one for women who traveled for work and left children at home.

She made the tough decision not to marry and had other choices to think about. In 1975, Gee Gee left the *Daily News* to become a columnist. The prospect seemed daunting, writing three columns a week and hoping that they'd be syndicated

widely enough for her to make a living. Her first syndicate editor mandated that Gee Gee couldn't write columns about foreign affairs or

Georgie Anne Geyer continues to watch and write about the world for American newspapers.
Courtesy of Georgie Anne Geyer

about women, until a sympathetic woman editor helped her slip them in. In time she felt free to write about whatever was on her mind. Time and travel had armed her with the ability to write knowledgeably about nearly anything.

Now free to live where she wished, Gee Gee moved to Washington and adopted a stray a cat for company. Pasha, "a direct descendant of the Egyptian godcats," so enthralled Gee Gee that she wrote a book about these handsome creatures who populate an independent feline world. In 1983 she wrote on a different subject: herself. In *Buying the Night Flight*, Gee Gee recounted the story of her childhood and the first 25 years of her career as a correspondent. She took her title from Antoine de Saint-Exupéry's *Night Flight*, a classic tale of a man facing his fears and the "sense of serenity and sovereignty and peace" that one must earn after making the hard choices that life brings.

Georgie Anne Geyer has continued to write about the world from places such as Vietnam, Iraq, Iran, and Afghanistan. Point to a spot on the map where the United States was fighting some kind of war, and Geyer would be there. Over the years, she would write more than 10,000 newspaper columns, distilling her observations and conclusions into 700 words each.

As of her 78th year, when this book was written, Georgie Anne Geyer was still writing three columns per week. When she looked back on her long career, certain memories stood out:

Strange things. Meeting a wonderful Panamanian couple, he the editor of the greatest paper in Panama and driven into exile by [Manuel] Noriega, in a dining room after Noriega fell, and laughing and crying with them. Watching my favorite country, Oman, come from a desert-full of nothing in 1978 to such intelligent development today that, in October of 2011, I attended the opening of Sultan

Qaboos' Royal Opera House with Plácido Domingo conducting. Seeing China changing before my eyes after 1984. Watching the Berlin Wall come down and Eastern Europe, freed, and seeing the "Great Communist Empire" in shards. Seeing Lebanon at the height of its beauty in the early '70s. Getting through to Fidel Castro, Saddam Hussein and the Guatemalan guerrillas—most of all, it is this joyous sense of doing something that no one else has or can do, of breaking through walls and barriers, of speaking other languages as though you were a bird in flight. And bringing it all home to my paper and my people.

6

A Challenge
That Never Ends
1990–Present

Early in 1992 the United States and European community recognized the newly independent nation of Bosnia and Herzegovina, formerly part of communist Yugoslavia. The small country was home to three ethnic groups with ties to people in other Balkan nations: Croats (Roman Catholic Croatians), Serbs (Orthodox Serbians), and Muslims known as Bosniaks.

Within days Serbian paramilitary forces launched artillery attacks on Sarajevo, Bosnia's lovely capital, and blockaded the city. The Bosnian Serbs, assisted by Serbs from the Yugoslavian army, embarked on a murderous program of genocide, what they called "ethnic cleansing" as they drove Bosnia's Muslims from their homes across two-thirds of Bosnia. More fighting arose when Croats and Bosniaks also turned on each other in 1992, but their battles ended early in 1994 when they agreed to peace terms. However, the Serbs kept fighting.

The 1995 Dayton Peace Accords established a framework for peace among the Republic of Bosnia and Herzegovina, the Republic of Croatia, and the Federal Republic of Yugoslavia. United Nations forces arrived to enforce the peace agreement, especially among Serb forces who resisted. The Serbs kept up their siege of Sarajevo until February 1996.

Late in the 1990s, ethnic Albanians called Kosovars (mostly Muslims who lived in the Serbian province of Kosovo) formed the Kosovo Liberation Army to create an independent Kosovo. The Serbian Orthodox Church has many sacred sites based in Kosovo, and Serbia considered the province vital to its sovereignty. The Kosovars carried out attacks against Serbian police stations, and in 1998, the Serbian government responded with a wave of ethnic cleansing against the Kosovars.

The United States recognized Kosovo as a nation in 2008, but China and Russia have not.

Janine di Giovanni

REPORTING FROM SARAJEVO AND KOSOVO

When I look at war, I don't see military strategies. I see it from the micro level: how is this affecting families, schools, hospitals? I think of supply routes and water tanks and how people get through a winter without electricity and antibiotics.

—Janine di Giovanni

Sometimes a kid just feels different, that she doesn't fit in. She grows up in a big New Jersey family with seven children. As she gets older, she starts to realize that her family has secrets and doesn't talk about unpleasant things, such as the sister who died 10 years before the girl was born or the brothers who hide their drugs in the attic. After all, if you don't talk about problems, then they don't exist.

But Janine di Giovanni, the last child born into her family in the mid-1960s, didn't want to live a life denying things. Plus she wanted to learn as much as she could about other people. She started by writing a high school research paper on the Hopi Tribe of Arizona. She knew she had a gift for writing, so she went to study English at the University of Maine. Like a painter with brush to canvas or a singer who masters a tricky passage of music, her passion was to create—with words on a page.

After graduating, she was awarded a slot in the Iowa Writers' Workshop, a coveted spot awarded to only 40 writers each year. But life in Iowa was a lonely existence—she was far younger than her classmates, many of them published authors with long lists of books to their credit, and the competition and petty jealousies discouraged her. She quit the program, taking with her one key discovery: writing, she learned, is an "isolated profession. You're going to spend a lot of time by yourself and face a lot of rejection." Somewhere along the line she got the idea to be a foreign correspondent.

Janine moved to Boston and got a job as a beat reporter at a local paper covering the daily round of fires, checking the police blotter, and writing up the dry but vital reports of council meetings and school board news. She faced years of working her way up the ladder toward becoming a foreign correspondent for a US news outlet, so she made a jump. In Europe, she decided, there was an appreciation for people like her, individuals who were "eccentric and out-of-the-box as opposed to the United States where people are far more conventional." So she moved. She and her then-husband, a photographer, set up house in London. Janine talked an editor into paying for her airfare, and she flew to Israel to get her first story as a foreign correspondent, talking with Palestinians who were in revolt against the government. Europe gave Janine the chance to "live the life of a writer," and she became a British citizen. Her marriage broke up, and free of anything to keep her feeling tied down, she left for Sarajevo, Bosnia, in December 1992, where the Serbian army had laid siege to the Bosnian civilians who lived in the ancient capital city. Sarajevo, once a glorious Old World city and host to the 1984 Winter Olympics, was also home to a cosmopolitan mix of Roman Catholics, Serbian Orthodox Christians, and Muslims who had worked together and lived in the same neighborhoods for years.

But the neighboring country of Serbia was on the march, determined to "cleanse" Sarajevo of its Muslim citizens. The Serbian Army had turned the city into a wasteland. Water lines ran dry. Electricity was unreliable. Food disappeared. Children, cooped up indoors for days on end, ran outside to play, and died, shot by Serb snipers. Janine arrived to see a Sarajevo in agony. WELCOME TO HELL, the graffiti greeted her as she was driven into Sarajevo. It was hell, indeed.

She stayed there for months. It was not lost on her or any other reporter in Sarajevo that genocide was taking place in Bosnia. They asked themselves how Europeans and their governments could allow this to happen. The Nazi Holocaust against Europe's Jews had unfolded fewer than 50 years before.

As Serbian artillery pounded Sarajevo from the mountainsides that surrounded the city, Janine moved into the Holiday Inn in downtown Sarajevo. It was hardly a hotel—half the building was a shot-out shell—but a hardened news corps contingent lived there, reporters for big-name newspapers and magazines, photojournalists, TV reporters, producers, and cameramen, plus an assortment of independent journalists such as Janine, who made a living going from war to war to get interviews and sell the stories to media outlets.

It was freezing cold. Most of the time the Holiday Inn had no heat, electricity, or running water. At night, Janine lit a candle in her fourth-floor room and typed her stories on a battery-charged word processor. Once per week she swapped packs of Marlboro Lights for a pail of hot water she hauled up the steps to her room so she could wash her hair. She and the assortment of reporters, camera crews, and producers who lived in the Holiday Inn ate rice and cheese scrounged from humanitarian food deliveries. Sometimes dinner was chocolate bars and whiskey. To entertain themselves, the more daring hotel guests rappelled from the top floors of the hotel into the lobby below.

The Holiday Inn sat at the end of a street nicknamed Snipers' Alley, and when carloads of journalists went to work, they roared out of the hotel's underground garage at full speed to avoid getting shot. Janine was an indie journalist without a car, and she begged rides with TV journalists whose staff always had armored cars. "CNN's truck was always full," she recalled, "and they had the reputation of helping no one but their own. The BBC people, however, were more generous, and they usually waved me into the back of their truck. 'Get in, hurry up.' The back of the car smelled of gasoline from the stores of petrol in tin cans."

Then one hot August day she got the nod to go to Zuc, the battle line where the final battle to defend Sarajevo on Gogo Brdo, Naked Hill, took place.

And during those long, hot August days, there were dead men on Naked Hill. Most of them were very young. They

were soldiers, they had been killed, and it was too dangerous to remove their bodies. And so they lay where they
fell, in the shimmering heat. The men who came down
from the trenches for resupply every few days said the
smell of the dead wafted down into the trenches where
the living cowered, waiting for the next round of gunfire.
I did not know what the dead smelled like when they rotted in the sun, but a year later, in Rwanda I would understand it: I would see rows and rows and rows of bodies,
the dead mothers holding their children stiffened by rigor
mortis, fathers with their eyes melting from the heat, and
I would remember again Naked Hill.

The siege of Sarajevo and the war in Bosnia affected Janine di
Giovanni in a way no future war zones ever would. Janine, who
twice met the legendary war correspondent Martha Gellhorn,
learned an essential piece of wisdom about the life she had cho-
sen: "Martha Gellhorn once wrote about loving only one war
and the rest being duty. I still feel like that—Bosnia was the war
that took and broke my heart in a million little pieces."

In Bosnia, Janine met hundreds of hungry, suffering people,
families who had lost parents, grandparents, and children. The
desperation of the very young and the very old—the truly help-
less—especially grabbed at her heart. She befriended several,
including Nusrat, a small Muslim boy living in an orphanage,
and Zlata Filipovic, a 13-year-old girl whose wartime diary was
the talk of journalists—they called her the "Anne Frank of Sarajevo." When the diary was published in English in 1994, Janine
wrote an introduction recalling the days she spent with Zlata
and her family—how Zlata's mother, a chemist before the war,
was slowly going mad; how the family hid in a "safe room"

when the Serbs shelled their neighborhood; how Zlata pointed to the snapshot of her standing with a small friend who was killed, a gesture of remembrance.

It was also in Bosnia that Janine fell in love with a French television cameraman named Bruno Girodon. They had no real future together—their jobs took them to far-flung corners of the world—and the handsome Frenchman with the bewitching green eyes had a longtime girlfriend who, when she learned about Janine, insisted that he never contact Janine again.

Janine moved on. She turned 30, 32, and then 35, earning her living by traveling to war zones to speak with the people caught between opposing sides and telling their stories in magazines and newspapers across Europe and North America. One could track her travels by the articles and books she wrote, long pieces for *Vogue*, *Vanity Fair*, and the *Times of London* Sunday edition, reporting from Bosnia, Lebanon, Israel, Iraq, Pakistan, Afghanistan, Zimbabwe, and Sierra Leone. The titles of her books speak of the life she led—*Against the Stranger: Journeys Through Occupied Territory*; *The Quick and the Dead: Under Siege in Sarajevo*; *Madness Visible: A Memoir of War*; *The Place at the End of the World: Stories from the Frontline*.

Then, in 2003, she ran into Bruno Girodon again. The old fires still burned. He asked her to marry him and have a baby, and she agreed. Janine wore a sleeveless, tea-length dress and white gloves at their wedding, which took place in a small Catholic church in the south of France. Then she and Bruno parted ways—he had work to do in Africa, and Janine, pregnant, wanted to make a trip to Jerusalem to interview Palestinians who were caught up in the second intifada, another uprising against Israel. When she got to Jerusalem, her own life turned upside down as she began to have troubles with her pregnancy.

One Israeli doctor warned her that she must stay in bed; a second doctor said that it was safe for her to go home to London for surgery and wait out the pregnancy there.

She packed up and left for London, had the surgery, and late in her pregnancy, she and Bruno moved to Paris where they planned to raise their child. Baby Hugo arrived in the spring, early but healthy. Now Janine craved a "bubble of happiness," a safe and perfect place where she, Bruno, and little Hugo could nest together. But that bubble flew away, far from her grasp.

Janine began to feel fear, as some new mothers do, and developed a ferocious need to protect her baby at all costs. She behaved as though she lived in a war zone instead of safe in her Paris home, which Bruno had so lovingly built for her. She hoarded cash, wrote out escape plans, and stuffed her diaper bag as if she were heading on a long, dangerous journey. Any stranger presented a possible threat. Born a Catholic, Janine went into churches and lit candle upon candle, praying for her dead father and dead brothers and praying that God would keep her little family safe. As she recuperated from an exhausting pregnancy and the first trying days of caring for a newborn, she also had to think about her future: Would she return to work as a foreign correspondent?

Janine needed to ask herself if she was addicted to the thrill of working from a war zone. Bruno urged her to go to work, assuring her that getting back in the field would help her to find out. In late summer of 2003, when Hugo was six months old, Janine flew into Iraq, where the US Army had removed Saddam Hussein from power that spring. She went to work in Sadr City, a slum outside Baghdad where insurgents had rebelled against the American military.

Janine learned a lot about herself on that trip. She missed her baby desperately, and an Iraqi official reminded her that she should not miss his first steps or lost tooth. But going through that experience braced her, and she returned to Paris sure that she wasn't addicted to her work in war zones. She made a well-considered decision: she would continue to work as she had before, but now she would cram into five days what would have taken a month to accomplish before.

Then their lives changed again. After Hugo was born, Bruno's back failed him, and he suffered for months. One day he left for a doctor's checkup and didn't come home. Janine received a phone call that threw her into confusion.

"He's suicidal," the doctor told her. Janine could not believe what she'd heard. Bruno was in a psychiatric unit. When she got him on the phone he said to her, "I'm so tired." Several weeks passed until he came home from rehab.

Like her husband, Janine had watched people suffer. Bad memories stayed with her, especially the pain or loneliness of children. The first time she had watched a gravely injured child crawling on a cot, she had gone outdoors and vomited. Yet over time Janine had disciplined herself when she was on the job to watch, ask questions, and take notes. Only when she was alone would she allow herself to cry, hold her head in her hands, or just stare at the ceiling.

When she returned from a war zone she did not talk about the places she'd been. She didn't like questions about how many dead bodies she'd seen or whether she'd been raped. Her memories "went into black bound notebooks and the notebooks went into a box and the box went into the basement. From there, I could look at them someday and remember all the people, the places, the red dirt, the rain, and the mud. But for now, I was fine. I always thought Bruno was too."

A psychiatrist had told Janine that her resilience and her writing had helped her to cope with the horrors she witnessed. She wasn't a candidate for post-traumatic stress disorder (PTSD). Bruno, however, wasn't built the same way. Like warriors returning from the battlefield, he suffered from PTSD. It was not just physical pain that plagued him; he was having a mental breakdown. Bruno Girodon had watched human suffering through the lens of his television camera for 20 years, and it had taken its toll. He tried to cope with his illness by rehabbing a new flat for Janine and their son, working like a madman in spite of the discs disintegrating in his back.

Janine learned that five times as many war correspondents as ordinary people exhibit signs of PTSD after living and working in such frightful settings. Bruno showed every one. He was deep into depression. He couldn't sleep and spent entire nights

Janine di Giovanni, Bruno Girodon, and their son Hugo. *Courtesy of Janine di Giovanni*

drinking bottles of wine and listening to jazz. Clearly he was an alcoholic, but for the time, Janine couldn't confront that fact as she watched her husband crumble in front of her. Denial was a family tradition; the di Giovannis didn't talk about unpleasant matters. Not until Bruno was nearly arrested for driving drunk could Janine shake herself loose and confront the grim fact that her husband was an addict.

Bruno reentered rehab and then joined Alcoholics Anonymous to help himself manage his illness. He became so obsessed with AA that he practically abandoned Janine and their child for those he met at AA. They separated, agreeing that Hugo would have both of them in his life. Janine makes sure that her son is in the safe, loving care of his father or his nanny when she goes to the field.

Many would question how she could leave her son for such dangerous work, but Janine felt that her work was equal to her responsibility at home. Now, a decade later, Janine continues her mission: to bear witness to scenes of war so that readers can grasp the grim reality of how ordinary people live amid bombs and bullets and to give these forgotten a voice.

When the work demands it, she travels. When she's home and her son is at school, she researches, interviews, and writes from their flat in Paris. She is their breadwinner, living what she calls a "hand-to-mouth existence," though Janine admits it's a "privileged" way to earn her living.

She receives enormous satisfaction from doing what she loves. As much as she has loved her child's father, she "never wanted to be dependent on a man," she said. "When my father died, my mother didn't know how to write a check." Her dry humor came over the phone as she spoke of a woman friend, a banker who stated flatly, "I never want a man to buy my knickers."

Janine di Giovanni reported from Helmand Province when the United States and Great Britain were at war in Afghanistan. *Courtesy of Janine di Giovanni*

Janine di Giovanni continues to board international flights that take her to the world's most dangerous places. After the Arab Spring in December 2010 launched a series of revolutions and revolts, she traveled into Syria, Egypt, and Libya. She contributes to television and radio news on three continents; Americans hear her on NPR and PBS. Her articles appear in German, French, British, Canadian, and American newspapers including the *New York Times*, the *Sunday Times* (London), the *Guardian*, *Newsweek/Daily Beast*, *Vogue*, and *Harper's Bazaar*.

Troubles in the Middle East

For thousands of years, history has told of continuing war in the Middle East. After World War II, Britain granted independence to territories throughout most of its colonial empire and signed Palestine over to the United Nations in 1947. In turn, the UN announced plans to partition, or divide, Palestine into two states: one as a Jewish homeland for settlers and Holocaust survivors; the other, a state for Muslim Arabs. In May 1948, the Jews established the state of Israel. Jerusalem, sacred to Jews, Christians, and Muslims, stayed divided. And the issue of a homeland for Palestinians was left hanging.

Since 1948, a series of wars between Israel and its Arab neighbors has kept the region in turmoil. In 1988, Yasser Arafat, chief of the Palestinian Liberation Organization (PLO), reversed his position and acknowledged Israel's right to exist. Six years later, the PLO and Israel reached an understanding, but the violence has continued. A Palestinian nation has never been established.

WARS WITH IRAQ AND AFGHANISTAN

Iraq invaded its small neighbor Kuwait in August 1991, touching off a series of events that led to the Persian Gulf War. The United States, in tandem with its allies in NATO (North Atlantic Treaty Organization), responded with air strikes against Iraqi military installations and oil fields in January 1992. The Allies crushed Iraq's military, but its dictator, Saddam Hussein, stayed in power until he was captured during the Iraq War late in 2003.

The September 11, 2001, terrorist attacks on the United States forever changed the American nation. Within weeks the US military invaded Afghanistan to hunt for Osama bin Laden, leader of a Muslim terrorist organization called al-Qaeda, as well as to overthrow the Taliban, Afghanistan's ultraconservative Islamic government.

AN ARAB SPRING

Most of the world was caught off guard in 2010 when a young man named Mohamed Bouazizi set himself on fire to protest institutional corruption in Tunisia. This act sparked the over-throw of his government and others across the Arab world and was quickly tagged the "Arab Spring." At issue for Arab nations is whether they can evolve into Islamic democracies or whether they will succumb to ultraconservative Muslim governments who base their laws on a very narrow interpretation of the Koran. Foreign correspondent Robin Wright is among the jour-nalists traveling throughout the Middle East to study and inter-pret the matter.

Robin Wright

REPORTING FROM ANN ARBOR,
ANGOLA, BEIRUT, AND CAIRO

The Islamists are not only coming. In several countries, they've already arrived.—Robin Wright

In the 1950s, sets of orange-covered biographies of famous women lined library shelves across the America. With large print and characters illustrated in solid black silhouettes, these kid-friendly books drew boys and girls to sit down and read them cover to cover. There was *Dolly Madison: Quaker Girl* and others on Florence Nightingale, Harriet Beecher Stowe, and Amelia Earhart. A set stood on a library shelf in Ann Arbor, Michigan, where a schoolgirl named Robin Wright devoured every one. Like the hundreds of people she went on to inter-view and write about in the next 50 years, these women became part of her journey. Robin Wright wanted to be like one of these women, "women who had done things on their own."

Robin Wright grew up in a family that liked to ask questions. Both of her parents were academics who encouraged her to follow her own path. Her mother, Phyllis, had followed her own muse: she had danced with Agnes de Mille as a young woman and was still in community theater with a role in *The Vagina Monologues* at the age of 91. Robin's father, L. Hart Wright, taught his law students using the Socratic Method: series of questions and answers—always to be followed by another question.

At suppertime, her father quizzed Robin and her sister about current events and the world in general. Much was going on—the Cold War between the United States and the Soviet Union had spawned crisis after crisis, even as Third World countries in Africa, Asia, and the Middle East were fighting wars of independence. At the dinner table, the Wrights played "geography," tossing out names of countries from Burma to Zambia, as well as the add-a-letter-to-make-a-word game "three-thirds of a ghost." But these dinner table games extended to another serious subject: the brawling world of big-league sports. In the Wright household, sports held equal weight, and Hart Wright loved them all. He schlepped his daughters to college games and filled their heads with scores and stats. Robin grew up knowing her state and world capitals, and she could talk baseball, basketball, and football for hours.

Many kids who grew up reading those orange-covered biographies went on to study history at the University of Michigan, and Robin was one of them. She had absolutely no plans to become a journalist until she had a happy accident. A sorority sister suggested she write for the *Michigan Daily*, the nation's biggest college newspaper, which ran six days a week with 24- and 36-page issues. Robin told herself, "Maybe I'll go off and join the paper and write an article about sports just as a joke to my father." She ended up "loving it" and joined the *Daily's* sports page. By her senior year in 1969, Robin Wright had worked her way up to become the first female sports editor of a student paper in the United States.

The year 1969 was a turbulent one for American students and Americans in general. Bitter protests against the Vietnam War gripped the Michigan campus. But as hot as the political scene was in Ann Arbor, there was other news to cover. Michigan's ailing football team had a new coach, Bo Schembechler, and he was turning things around. Robin traveled with the team to Saturday games at Big Ten stadiums, and she had a quiet deal with the players: in return for not following them into the locker room—in 1969 it was unthinkable for women sportswriters to interview players as they showered and dressed—they promised to save some comments just for her. Come Monday morning, *Daily* readers opened the sports page for an exclusive bit of news by Robin Wright.

On New Year's Day 1970, as Michigan played in the Rose Bowl, Robin did her part to break the gender barrier in sports reporting. As she made her way to the press box, two sheriff's deputies blocked her from entering. True to form, the only women allowed in the press box were there to serve food or send Western Union teletypes updating the game. But Wright had a scoop—a U of M player had shared important news with her. That morning, Coach Schembechler had had a heart attack. "I was the only one who had information about the best story of the day," Robin recalled years later, but she had no way to share it. "The boys in the press box knew I always had good stories," so she sent them a note about her predicament. In support, "the entire male press corps got up and walked out." Nervous Rose Bowl officials quickly saw they weren't going to get any press coverage at all, and they let her in.

Wright earned both her bachelor's and master's degrees in history at Michigan. When she cast about for a summer internship, there weren't any in history, so she took one from the *Christian Science Monitor*, a national newspaper based in Boston. Again, she loved it, another happy accident. But for a young woman who had read those orange biographies, her choice of a career made sense. Robin Wright became one of those women who did things on her own.

Almost from the start, Robin reported from overseas when she moved to Africa, first for the *Monitor*, later for the *Washington Post* and for *CBS Evening News*, when she learned the art of reporting in front of a camera. For seven years in the 1970s, she witnessed the violence that accompanied change as old governments fell and new ones rose. She covered revolutions, interviewed dictators, and watched bloody uprisings as black South Africans rose up against apartheid. Robin got the first story about the murder of black South African Steve Biko, an activist with two small boys, who was "arrested and detained" by the white government and died in prison after being beaten by his police interrogators. She recalled how she "broke the story about Steve Biko when he died. I got in to see his body after he'd been brutalized, and I got the pathologist's report about how he really died . . . one of the biggest scoops as a young journalist." In return, the South African government tried to get her expelled.

A small quote taped to her monitor reads, "The things you are scared of are the most worthwhile." "The fact is I'm afraid of a lot of things: elevators and airplanes . . . I'm not brave," Robin said flat out. "I'm actually hideously afraid of things like war and being in war zones. You never overcome fear, but when I think about the privilege of seeing history play out in front of me, [it] has made that fear worthwhile." Critics sarcastically tagged young women reporters like her as "mercenary groupies."

Her job was rarely easy and sometimes dangerous. She occasionally needed financial backing to work, and in 1976 she won a fellowship from the Alicia Patterson Foundation to study the dismantling of Portugal's African empire. She went to Angola to report on five British mercenaries, regular "blokes" lured from day jobs as factory workers and bricklayers with the promise of tax-free dollars as soldiers of fortune in Africa. They commanded a pro-democracy militia in a small town but had no ammunition to defend themselves.

Early in 1976, Robin found the mercenaries in the tiny town of Santo Antonio do Zaire at the Angola-Zaire border, where the Congo River poured into the Atlantic Ocean. Angolan forces, backed by Cuban troops, stormed the town with a tank and machine guns. Civilians and soldiers ran for their lives.

Robin's first-hand report of the attack appeared in the *Christian Science Monitor* on February 9, 1976.

This reporter was present during the surprise assault on the coastal city, which is the northernmost point before the Zaire border.

The attack began at 8:45 AM, Feb. 6, with the sound of T-54 Soviet tanks and the crash of mortars falling on the hospital and airfield on the outskirts of town. At first many people thought the sounds were thunder from the gale-force of the rainy season that was drenching this steamy little town located six degrees below the equator.

There had been no warning of the attack . . .

Within seconds of the first shellings, the entire town was in chaos. People and troops fled down the street toward the river, the only exit on the peninsula.

At the port where half a dozen fishing boats were docked, women and children were fighting and pulling each other out to get a place.

. . . This reporter and one mercenary headed for the single small motorized boat that had just been repaired the night before. Approaching the vessel—smaller than a tiny tugboat—we saw it, too, was swarming with people clawing for space.

Of the 350 people in that small town, 22 made it out alive, including Robin and the two mercenaries. The attackers slaughtered the rest.

Robin returned to Angola when three captured mercenaries went on trial, and the revolutionary government tried to call her as a witness. She refused to testify, on the grounds that she was a journalist, not a participant in the fighting. Accusing Robin of spying for the CIA (the Central Intelligence Agency), the Angolans put her in prison, which she described as "a memorable week." In 1977, she won the Overseas Press Club award for the best reporting in any medium requiring exceptional courage and initiative.

In 1980 Robin moved to Rome. Often the only woman on the plane, she traveled with Pope John Paul II as he faced down a military dictatorship in Brazil and Ferdinand Marcos, the corrupt president of the Philippines. The next year she moved to Beirut, Lebanon's capital city. Once known as the "Paris of the Middle East," Beirut had been leveled to rubble during Lebanon's civil war. Robin made Beirut her home for five years. She reported on Israel's invasion of Lebanon in 1982 and watched the rise of Hezbollah, a Shiite Muslim terrorist organization backed by Iran. In the early hours of October 23, 1993, she was awakened by a huge explosion five or six miles distant: a suicide bomber had driven a truck loaded with explosives into a barracks and killed 241 US Marines as they slept. As of 2014, the bombing represented the single worst attack on a group of American military since World War II.

The years moved on, and Robin grew to learn more and more about life in the Middle East. She talked with hundreds of people on the streets of Lebanon, Egypt, Syria, Iran, Iraq, Libya, Morocco—virtually every Middle Eastern nation. She already spoke French, widely used in the Middle East and North Africa, but she regretted she didn't know more Arabic or Farsi (the Persian language spoken by Iranians) so she could better understand the people she met. She started to look at current events in mathematical terms. "If you know enough about a region, then it becomes like a mathematical equation. You figure what all the numbers are, and you figure out the solution. . . . Then, if something changes, there's a new variable. You throw in that factor and there's a new outcome."

Robin Wright makes regular appearances before college crowds to discuss developments in the Middle East.
Courtesy of Sam Colt

In late 2010 a new, shocking variable changed the equation in the Middle East when a young man named Mohamed Bouazizi set himself on fire to protest corruption in Tunisia, an act that sparked the Arab Spring. The sight of women and men filling the streets of Tunisia, Egypt, Libya, Yemen, Bahrain, and Syria caught Western governments off guard. But to Robin, the Arab Revolution was no surprise; she had seen it coming for years. "All the change in the world—the end of Communism in Eastern Europe, the end of apartheid and minority rule in Africa, the end of military dictatorships in Latin America—has all been part and parcel of the same phenomenon, and that is globalization."

Equipped with her historian's view over the long term and a gift for words, Robin uses a journalist's skills to interpret events as they unfold. "All these events—including the Arab [Spring] uprising—it's all part of . . . the whole idea that we've come up with a form of government democracy that will play out in lots of different ways. Whether parliaments, presidents, what kind of parties run against each other—the idea is that the people have a right to participate. It's far from over; we're only at the beginning stages. But this is arguably the single most important change in 500 years since city-states became nation-states. Now we are taking that next big step with nation-states moving toward globalization."

In a powerful piece she wrote in 2011, Robin told of one young woman's efforts at reform, Muslim-style, that have taken hold in Egypt and other Arab nations. Robin herself rarely wears a headscarf as she moves along the streets of the Middle East. However, her subject, Dalia Ziada, proudly wears the headscarf—hijab—as a sign of reform. Dalia is a member of Egypt's "Pink Hijab" movement, named for the vibrant headscarves that young Muslim women adopted as their symbol for women's and human rights in Egypt.

For many young women, hijab is now about liberation, not confinement. It's about new possibilities, not the past. It provides a kind of social armor that enables Muslim women to chart their own course, personally or professionally. For Ziada, hijab provides protective cover and legitimacy for campaigns she considers to be the essence of her faith—human rights and justice.

"Families feel much more comfortable allowing their girls to be active, to get higher education, or jobs, or even to go out alone at night when they are wearing hijab," [Ziada] told me. "It's a deal between a Muslim girl and society. I agree that I will wear hijab in order to have more space and freedom in return."

In its many forms, hijab is no longer assumed to signal acquiescence. It has instead become an equalizer. It is an instrument that makes a female untouchable as she makes her own decisions in the macho Arab world. It is a stamp of authenticity as well as a symbolic demand for change. And it is a weapon to help a woman resist extremism's pull into the past. Militants cannot criticize or target her for being corrupted by Western influence.

Robin Wright appears regularly on Sunday morning news programs and shares her expertise on television and radio broadcasts in the United States, Canada, United Kingdom, and Australia. She has written four books about Africa and the Middle East and has more to come. She chose a punk rock hit as the title for her 2011 book on democratic change in the Muslim world; *Rock the Casbah: Rage and Rebellion Across the Islamic World* relates how young Muslims are creating their own brand of Islamic democracy with hip-hop, comedy, poetry—and the pink hijab.

Following lives of ordinary people who rap and write poetry has been key to Robin's understanding of world events. "A lot of big-name correspondents like to swoop in and talk to top officials," she said, "but the danger is they live in a bubble that's divorced from reality. I really like getting out on the street and just talking to people." She notes that many of today's correspondents "do drop-bys . . . they come in for a couple weeks or months and go home." But that's not how she has lived her life or done her job.

She shares little about her private life. She never married, "not my choice," she emphasized. "I always thought I would, but you don't have time for everything and I'm not going to do something just for the sake of doing it. In the right situation it might have happened." That said, there have been special men in her life. "Interesting characters," she mused. She is much more open about her childhood, about her mother, who was an "inspiration," and her father, a veteran who would not tell his stories of World War II until Robin herself had experienced combat. Then, she said, they developed a whole new relationship, an almost unspoken understanding that they had a shared experience of war.

Robin said she fears that American kids today don't know enough about the world, especially because globalization will define their lives in the 21st century. Third World kids, she says, "do get it . . . they speak English and multiple languages. They probably know more about American geography than American kids."

For any young person thinking about a career as a foreign correspondent, Robin recommends learning everything possible about the world. "Know the world . . . and know the world *well*. Speak at least two other languages, only one being another European language and the other involving a whole different alphabet—Chinese, Russian, Japanese, Arabic—something to bridge the cultural gap."

Writing is only 5 percent of a journalist's job. "I tell young people, 'Don't major in journalism . . . you can learn those skills working on the student paper or taking a good writing class. Major in the field you want to cover. It requires an extraordinary amount of expertise to be able to understand what the truth is.

"A lot of young correspondents have a theory about what's happening and look for someone to give a quote that supports it . . . but you have to have a blank slate and carry out your own public opinion survey of what's *really* going on and how people *really* feel. It's not talking to five people; it's talking to hundreds of people . . . what's the public mood, [and] among officials, talk to all the different wings of government. . . . [It's] a much more daunting and demanding profession than most people understand."

Forty years as a working journalist and her depth of experience have earned Robin Wright recognition as a scholar in Middle Eastern issues. She flies to the Middle East regularly to observe and report on its changing politics and societies. She maintains a web page at robinwright.net, and she tweets from @wrightr.

THE MIDDLE EAST BEAT

Robin Wright isn't the only woman to specialize in Middle Eastern affairs. Women correspondents have long headed to the Middle East in search of the truth about what's going on there. Martha Gellhorn covered a Palestinian uprising, as did a younger reporter, Janine di Giovanni. Martha Raddatz has reported from there for both NPR and ABC News. Others include Christiane Amanpour, an Iranian by birth who made her name with American TV watchers on CNN during the Gulf War, and Marie Colvin, an American reporting for the *Sunday*

Times of London who was killed in Syria in 2012. There are more: NPR's Middle East correspondent Deborah Amos, CBS correspondent Martha Teichner, and CBS correspondent Kimberly Dozier, who was gravely injured in a 2006 car bombing in Iraq that killed everyone around her.

Martha Raddatz

REPORTING FROM THE PENTAGON, WHITE HOUSE, BAGHDAD, AND KABUL

The one reason more than any other that I love the news business is because I learn something every single day. Every single day.—Martha Raddatz

About 9 PM EDT on Sunday evening, May 1, 2011, Americans were getting ready for the week, thinking about Monday morning and going back to work or school. Some in the East and Midwest sat down to tune in to *Desperate Housewives* or *The Amazing Race* when reports trickled in that the president was preparing to speak to the nation—a most unusual event for a Sunday night.

ABC News foreign correspondent Martha Raddatz was sitting on an airplane waiting to take off on a long, tiring flight to Afghanistan, one of many she'd made since the United States had gone to war there in 2001. Her BlackBerry phone buzzed, and the next thing she knew, she was off the plane, her luggage retrieved, sitting on the floor of a terminal at Washington Dulles International Airport talking on two phones at once. She'd gotten a tip—probably the biggest of her professional life. Osama bin Laden, mastermind of the September 11 attacks on the United States, had been shot dead by a select team of American soldiers at his hideaway compound in a Pakistani city. Martha spoke to her son, at home with friends, knowing that he'd be worried not just about his mom but also about what was going on. She swore him to secrecy, shared the news, and emphasized that he tell no one. (He complied.) Then she got back to work. Raddatz, an on-camera reporter, is one of the most visible parts in the well-oiled machine that is ABC News, known to media types as a "news operation." It's an operation, all right: massive amounts of research and prior planning, copy written, videos shot and edited beforehand. There was new information, only hours old, gleaned from sources at the White House, the Pentagon, and the CIA—how the raid was kept secret, how the compound was laid out, who was living there, and how bin Laden died. Money was spent, lots of it, so that Raddatz and her ABC colleagues could get on the air with full coverage by 7 AM Monday. Americans were sure to tune in.

That morning Martha Raddatz gave a live report from the Pentagon. She stood in front of the memorial whose 184 benches, evoking the tail of a crashed airliner, stand in honor of the men and women killed when a terrorist flew a hijacked American Airlines plane into the Pentagon. As computer-generated images of bin Laden's compound appeared on screen, she reported on the logistics of killing him—"Bin Laden was ordered to surrender but refused. The SEALs shot him in the head, likely a double-tap, two shots to ensure a kill."

Martha Raddatz looked the complete professional as she reported from the Pentagon that morning—conveying information in the calm, purposeful manner that one expects from a veteran correspondent. She's an expert on so many aspects of the bin Laden story: the September 11 attacks on the United States, Middle Eastern politics, wars in Iraq and Afghanistan, the

US military, the White House, the Pentagon. Bin Laden's death was one endpoint—there will be more—of a long, complicated and never-ending news story, one that has taken Martha from Washington to Iraq, Afghanistan, and Pakistan so many times she has nearly lost count.

A career in TV news wasn't what she'd planned on. Martha grew up in Salt Lake City, Utah, a Protestant. Her father died before she turned three, and Martha's mother raised her and her sister. When she was a girl, Martha had "absolutely no inkling" what she wanted for a career, but her mom's Saturday morning trips to the library stand as a bedrock experience. She read—a lot. "I liked to read biographies," she recalled. "Maybe that's the first inkling you want to live a life that's not the one you're living."

She went to college at the University of Utah, with no firm grasp on career plans when opportunity knocked during her senior year and a job opened at a small TV station in Salt Lake. Martha dropped out of school and took the job, which on reflection she admitted "was stupid." She moved up from grunt-work tasks to shooting her own film (still part of the job at small stations) and going on camera when she was 24. She moved to Boston and instantly adored living there. She stayed for 12 years.

"Before she was Martha Raddatz at ABC News, she was Martha Bradlee here at Channel 5, WCVB-TV, and she was a heck of a reporter," wrote *Boston Globe* columnist Kevin Cullen. She married her first husband, Ben Bradlee Jr. (son of the legendary *Washington Post* editor Ben Bradlee), and they had a daughter, Greta. Martha's job at WCVB took her out of town and overseas frequently, but she was able to plan her travels ahead of time, which made her family life somewhat easier to balance. She and Greta's father divorced, and Martha married again, an attorney named Julius Genachowski, with whom she has a son, Jake. Jake was 10 when Martha started reporting from war zones. (Today Martha is married to NPR correspondent Tom Gjelten.)

Martha's interest in military issues expanded over those years. She left Boston to report from the Pentagon for NPR in 1993 and was drawn to the war in Bosnia during a horrendous time, when another woman correspondent, Christiane Amanpour of CNN, provided inspiration. "I remember thinking, 'Wow, that woman was so brave,'" she recalled. Martha went to Bosnia five times. Reporting on the US Department of Defense and the US military intrigued her. The Pentagon beat, a "microcosm of society," fascinated her. Martha understood that reporting from the Pentagon encompassed more than the nuts and bolts and bullets of making war. "It involved death," she explained. "It involved society's issues." The human dimension—stories of real men and women—compelled her to become an expert on the American military. This has taken more than 20 years. Like Georgie Anne Geyer, Martha has worked at building her "institutional memory" for decades. Like Geyer, she simply "knows what to do."

She moved to ABC in 1999, returning to work in front of the camera as a State Department correspondent. On June 22, 2001, she contributed to an ABC News report:

> US Navy warships have pulled out of Persian Gulf ports and a Marine Corps exercise in Jordan was halted following the detection of an "imminent" and specific terrorist threat against Americans, ABC News has learned. . . .
>
> And less than a month ago, four followers of Osama bin Laden, a wealthy Saudi exile suspected of sponsoring terrorism, were convicted of involvement in the 1998 bombings of two US embassies in Africa that killed 224 people, including 12 Americans.

Shortly after that verdict, on May 29, the US government issued a worldwide caution for Americans, warning intelligence had been received in early May that American citizens abroad might be the target of a terrorist threat from extremists linked to bin Laden's al-Qaeda organization.

US authorities also suspect bin Laden associates were involved in the attack on the *Cole*. [A suicide terrorist attack on the USS *Cole* when it was docked in Yemen killed 17 US sailors in October 2000.]

On the morning of September 11, 2001, Martha was at home in Arlington, Virginia, when the first airplane hit the World Trade Center in New York City. Tom Gjelten, reporting for NPR at the Department of Defense, rushed to the Pentagon. Martha hurried to her office in Washington, checking in with Greta at Amherst College and with Jake's school as well before she got to the State Department:

The State Department was being refurbished so the press was in a downstairs temporary facility with one large TV. My young producer, Phuong Nguyen, was already glued to the images. Before we knew any details about where the planes came from, I remember thinking that no US pilot would ever fly into those buildings, even if there was a gun to his or her head, so I assumed that the planes must somehow [have] been stolen. Officials I was calling assumed the same.

Nothing made sense that day. And then less than 20 minutes after arriving at the State Department, there was a report of an explosion at the Pentagon. Just before we evacuated the State Department, it was confirmed that a plane had hit the Pentagon, although it was unclear on which side it had hit.

It was chaos outside. As soon as we were outside we heard reports there was a car bomb that had gone off at the State Department. I knew that was not true and reported that to ABC. Then Phuong and I walked to the Memorial Bridge, the one behind the Lincoln Memorial, and I looked across the river toward Virginia. A huge pillar of black smoke was coming from the Pentagon.

Martha wondered if Tom was all right, and then decided to be optimistic and assume, because news reports were coming from another part of the Pentagon, that he was OK.

I spent the day on that historic bridge watching the Pentagon burn, smelling it, and seeing fighter jets streaking down the Potomac. I knew I would not be back home for a very long time and that when I finally did [return], all of our lives would be changed.

The September 11 attacks on American soil also changed the direction of Martha's reporting. She got a transfer to the Pentagon in the spring of 2003, just as the United States went to war in Iraq, and embarked on a long series of visits there, sometimes to follow the defense secretary or generals as they inspected operations, and sometimes embedded with American soldiers as they carried out day-to-day operations in Mosul or Fallujah or to the desert in Al Anbar. "Embedded" was a new term in those days— a term coined to describe journalists who lived and worked alongside troops in a war zone, sharing meals and living spaces.

By the summer of 2004, matters had turned deadly for the Americans in Iraq as insurgents rose up against the military

Martha Raddatz and two US Marines in Ramallah, Iraq, in 2007. *Courtesy of Martha Raddatz*

with accusations that the United States had "occupied" Iraq. Martha, about to leave for home after a trip to Iraq, was having dinner with a group of generals when General Jack Keane shared details on a briefing he'd heard concerning a battle back on April 4. Eight soldiers had died that day after an attack in the Baghdad slum of Sadr City. A platoon from the First Cavalry Division, thinking they were on a peacekeeping mission, were caught in a "platoon pindown."

Martha expressed interest in doing a story for ABC's *Nightline* on the attack, but she was about to go back to Washington. The general offered his help, and two days later the army flew her to Sadr City, where a group of survivors awaited her. She later recalled this story for a reporter on C-SPAN.

I knew 8 soldiers had died, 60 were wounded. I sat down with these soldiers and it was one of the most incredible stories I've ever heard.

And it was a time I thought, OK, this is not policy. This is not the administration. This is these human beings who have been in this horrendous battle. And there was one in particular. There was this staff sergeant named Robert Miltenberger, who was sitting over in the side and kind of grumpy. And I thought, "This is the last thing this guy wants to do is talk to me." And they brought over Sergeant Miltenberger and he sat down. And I asked him one question about this, and he burst into tears and talked about how he'd had one hand on a sucking chest wound in one soldier. They were in back of the open truck, that he had the knee on the leg of another one. One of the soldiers was paralyzed, and he kept telling him he was OK.

And Sergeant—you could just see the pain in this man's face like I've never seen before. He was awarded a Silver Star for his heroics, all the time he's continuing to shoot.

There were others, Martha knew, the families at home at Fort Hood, Texas, who had gotten early word on the battle from CNN. Some would get the dreaded knock on the door from an Army chaplain and a fellow officer to provide official notification that their soldier had died. She knew there were family preparedness groups, networks of army wives on call to bring food and offer a shoulder to cry on to grieving wives and children.

Two months later, Martha was back in Iraq, again in Sadr City to do follow-up interviews with men from the First Cavalry. A second general, Peter Chiarelli, encouraged her to go to Texas to speak with families at home—a different story she could talk about on *Nightline*. Martha flew to Fort Hood.

Out of Martha's long talks with soldiers in Iraq, the wounded in hospitals, wives and parents at home, and army officials, came her book *The Long Road Home: A Story of War and Family*, published early in 2007. She didn't ask ABC for time off to write it, preferring to stay on the job and work into the wee hours to finish the manuscript.

Her book offers countless tiny details about the people whom Martha interviewed about the horrific attack, details that grieving people were willing to share. She took time to get to know them, to ask questions and to listen carefully. "No one asks them," she explained. "We say, 'What was it like? Did someone get killed?' And [we] don't really say, 'And then what happened? How did you find the courage? And how did you keep going on?'"

Her book garnered good reviews and a thumbs-up from a *New York Times* reviewer, whose skepticism about the freshness of the book—Martha's story had already played all over television—declared that *The Long Road Home* offered "searingly vivid evidence of the toll our soldiers pay." Others, including an antiwar columnist writing in the *Columbia Journalism Review*, questioned how she can maintain an objective view of the US military when she spends so much of her time living and working among its men and women.

Martha Raddatz states categorically that she can keep her reporter's objectivity even as she's embedded with US forces in spots like Iraq and Afghanistan. "I say things they don't want to hear," she once told an audience, "but I can never be objective about sacrifices and service. I have lost friends. I have had friends wounded."

Issues of personal safety are always in war reporters' minds, but it was rare for one to be attacked or killed in action until the past few decades, when journalists, producers, and photographers became fair game for enemy combatants. The Iraq War came home to ABC News in January 2006 when two of Martha's colleagues, coanchor Bob Woodruff and cameraman Doug Vogt, were gravely injured when a roadside bomb struck their military vehicle. And in February 2012, American journalist Marie Colvin, a veteran writer for the *Times* of London, was killed in Homs, Syria, reporting on the suffering of 28,000 civilians caught in Syria's civil war. One year earlier, CBS News reporter Lara Logan and her crew, including her producer, cameraman, and translator, were attacked in Cairo's Tahrir Square. The moment their camera battery lost its charge, a mob of men attacked. Logan was beaten and sexually assaulted, and nearly died.

"I think you take what safety precautions you can," Martha emphasized. "Bad things are going to happen. With Marie Colvin I don't think death had anything to do with her being a woman. She was the bravest journalist around, period. Lara's attack was horrendous, and I know she took precautions and had security men . . . you have to do what you can to mitigate that threat."

Lara Logan was criticized for leaving her two young children to report from a war zone. Martha Raddatz's kids are grown, but she has thought deeply about the issue. She is not sure she would have left them when they were little, and as teens, Martha said, they were more into their own problems than worried about hers. A smile stirred in her voice when she looked back on a trip to Bosnia when her daughter, Greta, was a young teen. Martha hadn't been in touch for two days. She set up a satellite phone to make a quick call home, and Greta answered. "Mom, thank God you called," she said. "I'm thinking of dropping Latin."

Of course, when children become young adults, their worries change. Years later, when Greta, by now working at the

Martha Raddatz (right) pictured with her ABC News producer, Ely Brown, in eastern Afghanistan. *Courtesy of Martha Raddatz*

University of California, Berkeley, got a call from Martha with the news of the explosion that injured Woodruff and Vogt. "My mom began to cry, and her tears fueled my own," Greta wrote. "I cried so hard I was gasping for air. I'd obviously heard the horror stories about journalists being wounded, kidnapped, and even murdered in Iraq. But this was different—it could easily have been her."

My mother's own experiences in Iraq have certainly made this war more meaningful for me. On Easter Sunday last year, my mom attended a sunrise church service at Camp Victory, the main military base in Baghdad. After the service, she flew out of Baghdad on a military cargo plane.

The following is an excerpt of an e-mail she sent that day:
"When we walked onto the plane, we saw in the middle four flag-draped coffins, stacked side by side. On the way home on Easter Sunday. The passengers were seated on the sides of them. Our luggage was next to the coffins. The retired general I was with walked back and touched the flags. I cannot describe how emotional it was to see those coffins so close to you, not knowing who they were but knowing how they probably died."

Martha Raddatz is appalled at the gap in understanding between the lives of everyday Americans and the soldiers who fight for the United States in places like Iraq and Afghanistan. "We've got a country that doesn't connect with the military . . . one in five are coming home with mental health issues and the suicide rate is *enormous*," she told a group of college students and their parents.

She points to the "war weariness" of Americans at home, where returning veterans and their families all too often fall through society's cracks. Multiple deployments—as many as three or four separate combat assignments—result in posttraumatic stress that plagues veterans throughout the ranks, from infantrymen on up to soldiers with stars on their shoulders. "One of the stresses we don't talk about is the stress on the generals, quite frankly," she said. "The horrible, horrible suicide rate" among the military is "an absolute crisis."

On a PBS program, Martha explained her concerns further:

Multiple deployments are so underappreciated by the American public. Sometimes they [returning servicemen and women] don't really engage when they come home. They can't . . . *I* have found that through the years, frankly. You're going back and forth, and you're in this horrible situation and you can't quite relate . . . when you come back, with friends or with your family because they weren't there.

Magnify that by a trillion times with these soldiers who are fighting, who are seeing the most horrific things that you can imagine, and then they're expected to come back and drive the minivan.

Martha Raddatz is now chief global correspondent for ABC News. In October 2012, she moderated the vice presidential debate between Vice President Joe Biden and Congressman Paul Ryan. The morning after the bombing at the Boston Marathon in 2013, she tweeted, "A crew from overseas on my plane to Boston to cover the attack. Usually it is me going overseas to cover their attacks." Follow her on Twitter at @MarthaRaddatz.

Afterword

You live in a world that moves faster every year. The notion of war correspondents packing typewriters, invading telegraph offices, broadcasting over huge microphones, or developing photographs in bathtubs may seem old-fashioned and irrelevant. Their world isn't your world. Mass communications (when I studied journalism in the 1970s, we mostly called it "the press")—the mix of daily newspapers, weekly and monthly magazines, and three national broadcast networks—has morphed into a frenzy of social media, the 24-hour news cycle, dying newspapers, and too many bloggers to count or read.

Yet, in the midst of this new, crazy communications medium we call cyberspace (new when you compare the past 15 or 20 years with 250-plus years of American journalism), *thinking* men and women must continue to ask, "What's real? What's not? Whose information do you trust?" Which is precisely what these 16 women asked of themselves and others as they worked as journalists in the field of war. "What's real? What's not? Whose information do you trust?"

If you picked this book up, you may well have an interest in news and current events, war, or history. Maybe you don't—and you read this for an assignment. Either way, there's something I think you should know.

You need to look for the truth. Throughout your life, whether you're in school, at work, or learning about something for the joy of it, you should ask the same questions these women asked. What's real? What's not? Whose information do you trust? Like any honest reporter, you must question what you read and hear. You must question sources who give you information and take time to think about their motivations and objectives. Good reporters do that. So must you.

—KLH

Notes

Chapter 1: World War I, 1914–1918

Henrietta Goodnough, aka Peggy Hull

"*It was July 4, 1917 . . .*": Wilda M. Smith, *The Wars of Peggy Hull: The Life and Times of a War Correspondent* (El Paso: Texas Western Press, 1991), 85.

"*wouldn't be caught dead . . .*": Ibid., 30.

"*a-shopping*": Ibid., 36.

"*'chief stunt . . . is to 'have things happen to her' . . .*": Ibid., 37.

"*I'm going to learn to shoot a rifle . . .*": Ibid., 40.

"*Wherever the army was . . .*": Ibid., 52.

"*little girls in red satin . . .*": Ibid., 54.

"*Units became separated . . .*": Ibid., 57.

"*Won't come back . . .*": *Muscogee Times-Democrat*, January 3, 1919.

"*Peggy always dressed . . .*": Irene Corbally Kuhn, *Assigned to Adventure* (Philadelphia: J. B. Lippencott, 1938), 159.

"*gray devils*": *The Wars of Peggy Hull*, 106.

"*undignified*": Ibid., 110.

"*When we've won . . .*": *Assigned to Adventure*, 112.

"*Peggy Hull, Nervy War* . . .": Ibid., 272.

"*If your only reason* . . .": *The Wars of Peggy Hull*, 136.

"*I attended two dances* . . .": *Deming Headlight*, January 10, 1919.

"*Siberia is on the threshold* . . .": *The Wars of Peggy Hull*, 144.

"*a monarchistically inclined* . . .": Ibid., 155.

"*China is worth the struggle* . . .": Ibid., 169.

"*Go to work* . . .": Ibid., 189.

"*The tenements crumbled* . . .": Ibid., 190.

"*crazed fury of a trapped* . . .": Robert Spiers Benjamin, ed., *Eye Witness* (New York: Alliance Book Corporation, 1940), 5, 8.

"*You know,*" he told her: Ibid., 13.

"*In a seemingly endless* . . .": Ibid., 8.

Louise Bryant, Bessie Beatty, and Rheta Childe Dorr

"*Whenever the firing* . . .": Rheta Childe Dorr, *A Woman of Fifty* (New York: Funk and Wagnalls, 1928), 339.

"*train deluxe* . . .": Bessie Beatty, *The Red Heart of Russia* (New York: Century, 1918), 6.

"*Peace, joy, exultation* . . .": Ibid., 17.

"*like a bone between two hungry dogs*": Ibid., 65.

"*Suddenly my wandering* . . .": Ibid., 66.

"*Ras dva tri chetiri* . . .": Ibid., 100.

"*soldier girl*": Ibid.

"*pushed them out* . . .": Ibid.

"*I love my gun* . . .": Ibid., 105.

"*simply have been* . . .": *A Woman of Fifty*, 365.

"*All the world knows* . . .": *The Red Heart of Russia*, 109.

"*factory men with* . . .": Ibid., 209.

"*great red arch* . . .": Ibid., 210.

"*go about*": Louise Bryant, *Six Red Months in Russia: An Observer's Account of Russia Before and During the Proletarian Dictatorship* (New York: George H. Doran, 1918), 267.

"*It is silly to defend . . .*": Ibid.

"*To have failed . . .*": *The Red Heart of Russia*, 480.

"*I saw a people . . .*": Rheta Childe Dorr, *Inside the Russian Revolution* (New York: Arno Press, 1970), 2.

"*[I] had not dared . . .*": *A Woman of Fifty*, 373.

"*had learned through . . .*": Ibid., 380.

"*seemed amused . . .*": Ibid., 382.

"*Her fans include . . .*": *Time*, September 21, 1942.

Helen Johns Kirtland

"*Mrs. Kirtland is the first . . .*": *Leslie's Illustrated Weekly Newspaper*, August 24, 1918.

"*Bride of L. S. Kirtland . . .*": *New York Times*, November 11, 1917.

"*try some photos*": Quoted in Beverly Brannen, "Helen Johns Kirtland (1890–1979)," biographical essay, Library of Congress.

"*I am first beginning . . .*": Ibid.

Chapter 2: Between World Wars: 1920–1939

Irene Corbally Kuhn

"*Turn the calendar . . .*": *Assigned to Adventure*, 432.

"*The girls and boys had . . .*": Ibid., 13.

"*craftsman who learned . . .*": Ibid., 15.

"*ink-stained company . . .*": Ibid., 16.

"*nose for news*": Ibid., 35.

"*short, bright*": Ibid., 42.

"*the stenographer's delight . . .*": Ibid., 63.

"*The war was over . . .*": Ibid., 73.

"*grammatical someplace else*": Ibid., 84.

"*new pert French . . .*": Ibid., 99.

"*scorched reminders . . .*": Ibid., 110.

"*We became so . . .*": Ibid., 148.

"*graphically ghastly*": Ibid., 115.

"*The standard requirements . . .*": *Los Angeles Times*, October 19, 1986.

"*so profound and . . .*": Ibid.

"*Work apart . . .*": *Assigned to Adventure*, 270.

"*I borrowed my terrified . . .*": Ibid.

"*paid for the baby*": Ibid., 271.

"*Promptly at two . . .*": Ibid., 312–13.

"*husband dangerously*": *Assigned to Adventure*, 352

"*Bert had been . . .*": Ibid., 354.

"*unknown causes*": Ibid., 354.

"*tremors of approaching . . .*": *Los Angeles Times*, October 19, 1986.

"*I couldn't leave . . .*": Irene Corbally Kuhn interview by Robert Cubbedge, November 20, 1969, Herbert Hoover Presidential Library, West Branch, IA.

"*please relay to San Francisco*": Doris Weatherford, *American Women During World War II: An Encyclopedia* (New York: Routledge, 2010), 254.

"*It was a sadistic . . .*": Irene Corbally Kuhn, "Tea and Ashes" in *Deadline Delayed* (New York: E. P. Dutton, 1947), 277.

"*victory* [which] *we let . . .*": Irene Corbally Kuhn, "Women Don't Belong in Politics," *The American Mercury*, August 1953, 3–6.

"*Your Child Is . . .*": *American Legion* magazine, June 1952.

"*Women Don't Belong . . .*": *American Mercury* magazine, August 1953.

"*You Ought to Get . . .*" : *American Mercury* magazine, November 1954.

Sigrid Schultz

"*Berlin, September 1 . . .*": William Shirer, *Berlin Diary: The Journal of a Foreign Correspondent, 1934–1941* (New York, A.A. Knopf, 1941), 193.

"*trotted by his . . .*": Sigrid Lillian Schultz, *Germany Will Try It Again* (New York: Neynal and Hitchcock, 1944), ix.

"*whose brain conceived . . .*": Ibid., 13.

"*take their orders . . .*": Ibid., 1.

"*Germany will try . . .*": Ibid.

"*Hitler grabbed my . . .*": Julia Edwards, *Women of the World: The Great Foreign Correspondents* (Boston: Houghton Mifflin, 1988), 64.

"*In 1930 I realized . . .*": *Germany Will Try It Again*, ix.

"*a treacherous betrayal . . .*": Ibid., 126.

"*as if exchanging . . .*": *Women of the World*, 66.

"*the newest toast . . .*": Nancy Caldwell Sorel, *The Women Who Wrote the War* (New York, Arcade Publishing, 1999), 64.

"*If Hitler says . . .*": Ibid.

"*the German people . . .*": *Germany Will Try It Again*, 86.

"*women would fight . . .*": Ibid., 131.

"*The first picture . . .*": Sigrid Schultz, "Angora: Pictorial Records of an SS Experiment," *Wisconsin Magazine of History* 50, no.4 (Summer 1967), 396.

"*the greatest threat . . .*", "One Who Warned of the Nazis," *New York Times*, March 13, 1977.

Dorothy Thompson

"*When I walked into . . .*", Dorothy Thompson, "I Saw Hitler," *Cosmopolitan*, March 1932, 32.

"*He is formless . . .*": Ibid., 33.

"*The cleanup was . . .*": *Harper's Bazaar*, December 1932, 50.

"*I approach life . . .*": Marion K. Sanders, *Dorothy Thompson: A Legend in Her Own Time* (Boston: Houghton Mifflin, 1973), 115–16.

"'These people are all crazy . . .'": Dorothy Thompson, "Goodbye to Germany," *Harper's Bazaar*, December 1932, 46.

"It was white . . .": Ibid., 50.

"Dorothy Thompson Expelled . . .": Frederick T. Birchall, "Dorothy Thompson Expelled by Reich for 'Slur' on Hitler," *New York Times*, August 26, 1934, 1.

"the opposition of the . . .": Peter Kurth, *American Cassandra: The Life of Dorothy Thompson* (Boston: Little, Brown, 1990), 425.

Although Dorothy's editors: Ibid.

Chapter 3: A Second World War: 1939–1945

"tremors of approaching . . .": Irene Corbally Kuhn, "Shanghai: The Way It Was: A Glance Back at a Short, but Extraordinary Era," *Los Angeles Times*, October 19, 1986.

Martha Gellhorn

"I think the world . . .": "The Outsiders: Martha Gellhorn," interview by John Pilger, 1983, video, 26:05, http://johnpilger.com/videos/the-outsiders-martha-gellhorn.

"so that she can buy . . .": Martha Gellhorn, "Chronicling Poverty with Compassion and Rage," *New Yorker*, January 17, 2013.

They stopped at a bar: Kenneth Schuyler Lynn, *Hemingway* (New York: Simon and Schuster, 1987), 465.

"After all, they have . . .": "Only the Shells Whine," *Collier's*, July 17, 1937, 64–65.

"The boy was shy . . .": Ibid., 49.

"would soon start . . .": Ibid., 64.

"Hurry, hurry, before . . .": Martha Gellhorn, *Travels with Myself and Another* (New York: Jeremey P. Tarcher/Putnam, 2001), 27.

"a face of black hate": Ibid.

"M. is going off . . .": Ibid., 32.

"small tatty planes": Ibid., 15.

"The passengers . . .": Ibid., 33.

"*a city shrouded*": Ibid., 35.

"*in a class . . .*": Ibid., 35.

"*Endurance*," Martha learned: Ibid., 35, 37.

"*were humane and civilized*": Ibid., 64.

"*He saw the Chinese . . .*": Ibid., 61.

"*Behind the barbed . . .*": Martha Gellhorn, "Dachau: Experimental Murder," *Collier's*, June 25, 1945, 16.

"*wounded, napalmed . . .*": Martha Gellhorn, "Combat Reporting," *Telegraph*, April 28, 2001.

"*all this objectivity . . .*": Ibid.

Sickened by what she saw: Martha Gellhorn, *The View from the Ground* (New York: Atlantic Monthly Press, 1988), 329.

"*The Muslim Arab attitude . . .*": Ibid., 293.

"*sexual scandal-mongering . . .*": "The War for Martha's Memory," *Guardian*, May 15, 2001.

"*Most of the media . . .*": John Pilger, "The Salacious Demolition Job on Martha Gellhorn Cannot Obscure a Remarkable Human Being," http://johnpilger.com/articles/the-salacious-demolition-job-on-martha-gellhorn-cannot-obscure-a-remarkable-human-being, accessed February 19, 2013.

Margaret Bourke-White

"*We climbed over . . .*": Margaret Bourke-White, *Portrait of Myself* (New York: Simon and Schuster, 1964), 18.

"*Wait*," *Father said*: Ibid.

"*plump and harmless . . .*": Ibid., 14.

"*that we both could . . .*": Ibid., 24.

"*silver-cord entanglement*": Ibid., 17.

"*You got him away . . .*": Ibid.

"*opened a dazzling . . .*": Ibid., 32.

"*smokestacks on the . . .*": Ibid., 35.

"*Don't worry about . . .*": Ibid., 35.

"*pictures and words . . .*": Ibid., 64.

"*ghostly patchwork . . .*": Ibid., 110.

"*Here in the Dakotas . . .*": Ibid., 110.

"*more heart and mind . . .*": Ibid., 136.

"*Then in the next . . .*": Ibid., 183.

"*most determined . . .*": Ibid., 183–84.

"*golden chains*": Ibid., 197.

"*invisible ink*": Ibid., 202.

Most military commanders: Ibid., 202.

"'*Hi, taxi!*'": Ibid., 211.

All the while, Margaret hugged: Ibid., 211.

"*Jesus Christ, they're . . .*": Ibid., 231.

Margaret was on her way: Ibid., 235–36.

"*sound of rushing wind . . .*": Ibid., 246.

"*grotesque routine*": Ibid., 246.

War could explain a lot: Ibid., 248.

"*We didn't know . . .*": Ibid., 258.

"*veil*": Ibid., 259.

"*made the most . . .*": Ibid.

Chapter 4: A Cold War: 1945–1989

Marguerite Higgins

"*Then suddenly, for . . .*": Marguerite Higgins and Carl Mydans, *War in Korea: The Report of a Woman Combat Correspondent* (New York: Doubleday, 1951), 107.

"*engaged in three . . .*": Carl Mydans, "Girl War Correspondent," *Life*, October 2, 1950, 57.

"*flabby routine of his . . .*": Marguerite Higgins, *News is a Singular Thing* (New York: Doubleday, 1955), 26.

"that she should . . .": Peter Noel Murray, "Marguerite Higgins: An Examination of Legacy and Gender Bias," (PhD diss.,

School of the University of Maryland, College Park, 2003), 88–89. DRUM (http://hdl.handle.net/1903/47).

"Marguerite is not so . . .": Ibid.

"bitchy little story": Keyes Beech, *Tokyo and Points East* (New York: Doubleday, 1954), 168.

"Korea was no . . ." War in Korea, 17.

"The road to Seoul . . .": Ibid., 19.

"Streams of retreating . . .": Ibid., 27.

"Are you correspondents . . .": Ibid., 78.

"We know now that . . .": Ibid., 16.

"What is more important . . .": Ibid., 58.

"I had already been . . .": Ibid., 99–100.

"there are no facilities . . .": Ibid., 97.

"further clarified his . . .": Ibid., 107.

"Ban on women . . .": Ibid., 107.

"I started to say . . .": Ibid., 126.

"Then, as the conviction . . .": Ibid., 127.

"At three o'clock . . .": Ibid., 141–2.

"Finally we pulled . . ." : Ibid., 143.

"The control ship . . .": Ibid., 143.

"Come on, you big . . ." : Ibid., 144–5.

"the warmth and new . . .": News is a Singular Thing, 248.

"For the simplest . . .": Ibid., 252.

"Despite her success . . .": Tokyo and Points East, 183.

Chapter 5: Ancient Peoples, Modern Wars

"South Vietnam represents . . .": "John F. Kennedy Speeches: Remarks of Senator John F. Kennedy at the Conference on Vietnam Luncheon in the Hotel Willard, Washington, DC, June 1, 1956," www.jfklibrary.org/Research/Research -Aids/JFK-Speeches/Vietname-Conference-Washington -DC-19560601.aspx.

Gloria Emerson

"Now Vietnam is our . . .": Gloria Emerson, *Winners & Losers: Battles, Retreats, Gains, Losses, and Ruins from the Vietnam War* (New York: Random House, 1976), vii.

"Gloria Emerson, an award-winning . . .": "Gloria Emerson Obituary," http://gloriaemerson.com/obit.pdf.

"And scoop a cloud . . .": Joyce Hoffman, *On Their Own: Women Journalists and the American Experience in Vietnam* (Cambridge, MA: De Capo Press, 2008), 23.

"allowed to go . . .": Craig R. Whitney, "Gloria Emerson, Chronicler of War's Damage, Dies at 75," *New York Times*, August 5, 2004, www.nytimes.com/2004/08/05/arts/gloria-emerson -chronicler-of-war-s-damage-dies-at-75.html.

"Even the Postcards . . .": Gloria Emerson, "Even the Postcards in Saigon Depict G.I.'s in Battle," *New York Times*, March 7, 1970.

"On Med-Evac Copter . . .": Gloria Emerson, "On Med-Evac Copter, Faces and Pain," *New York Times*, June 20, 1970.

build a truly sovereign: Gloria Emerson, "Buddhist Monks Quietly Lead Campaign Against Thieu," *New York Times*, September 3, 1971.

Once a Vietnamese woman: Gloria Emerson, et. al., *War Torn: Stories of War from the Women Reporters Who Covered Vietnam* (New York: Random House, 2002), xvi.

"warrior sense of revenge": Gloria Emerson. "Vietnamese General and a G.I. Who Want to See Victory," *New York Times*, February 17, 1971.

"Facts Invented for . . .": Gloria Emerson, "Facts Invented for a General's Medal," *New York Times*, October 21, 1970.

"To Company B . . .": Gloria Emerson, "To Company B, Apricots Suggest Death," *New York Times*, December 13, 1970.

"She [Gloria] jerked me by . . .": Judith Coburn, "Gloria Emerson,

May 19, 1929–August 4, 2004," http://gloriaemerson.com
/memorial_gloria.html.

"such a dark and . . .": *On Their Own*, 14.

She took on rock star: "John Lennon's Legacy," *The Notion* blog
on *The Nation*'s website, December 7, 2006, www.thenation
.com/blog/john-lennons-legacy.

"I could not rejoice" Maria S. Bonn, "The Lust of the Eye: Michael
Herr, Gloria Emerson and the Art of Observation," *Papers on
Language and Literature* 29, no. 1 (1993): 29–30.

"It's absolutely disgusting . . ."   : Rod Nordland, "Gloria Emerson, May 19, 1929–August 4, 2004," http://gloriaemerson
.com/memorial_gloria.html.

Georgie Anne Geyer

"Being from the South . . ." Georgie Anne Geyer, *Buying the Night
Flight: The Autobiography of a Woman Foreign Correspondent*
(New York: Delacorte Press, 1983), 120.

"For one reason . . .": Ibid., 282-83.

"simply knew *things"*: Ibid., 276.

"If you were not . . .": Ibid., 27.

"one of those suburban . . .": Ibid., 27–28.

"a very real bully . . .": Ibid., 27

"What if one person . . .": Georgie Anne Geyer, e-mail to author,
October 25, 2012.

"My choosing a profession . . .": *Buying the Night Flight*, 29–30.

"My family simply told . . .": Ibid.

"I particularly resented . . .": Ibid.

"Heroism had failed . . .": Ibid., 38.

"The Daily News *was also . . ."*: Ibid., 40.

"The mob went to a party . . .": Ibid., 42.

"The bishop of Chimbote . . .": Ibid., 50.

"In that languid scene . . .": Ibid., 56.
"every night we argued . . .": Ibid., 57.
"We—and only we . . .": Ibid., 58.
"What you have here . . .": Ibid., 60.
"I could take no chance . . .": Ibid., 73.
Castro exerted "mind control": Ibid., 78.
"You're not playing games . . .": Ibid., 5.
But the polite stranger . . . : Ibid., 5.
"puta": Ibid., 12.
A young guerilla startled: Ibid., 16.
After dinner with a friend: Ibid., 20.
"You learn what is real . . .": Ibid., 144.
"torment for any honest . . .": Ibid., 145.
"Dear, I'm surprised . . .": Ibid., 154.
"it would be around . . .": Ibid., 154.
"When I went to Latin . . .": Georgie Anne Geyer, e-mail to author,
    October 25, 2012.
"a whole wonderful . . .": Ibid.
"a direct descendent . . .": Buying the Night Flight, 327.
"sense of serenity . . .": Ibid., 287.
"Strange things . . .": Georgie Anne Geyer, e-mail to author.

Chapter 6: A Challenge That Never Ends

Janine di Giovanni

"When I look at war . . .": Janine di Giovanni, "Syria: When Non-
    violent Revolutions Spin Into Bloodshed," Newsweek, March
    11, 2013.
"isolated profession . . .": Janine di Giovanni, interview with
    author, September 25, 2012.
"eccentric and out-of-the-box . . .": Ibid.
"live the life . . .": Ibid.

But the neighboring country: *No Man's Land: Women Frontline Journalists*, written, produced, and directed by Shelley Saywell, for Bishari Film Productions Inc. in association with the Canadian Broadcasting Corporation (New York, NY: First Run/Icarus Films, 1994), VHS.

"CNN's truck was . . .": Janine di Giovanni, *Ghosts by Daylight* (New York: Alfred A. Knopf, 2001), 8.

"And during those long . . .": Ibid., 16–17.

"Martha Gellhorn once . . .": Janine di Giovanni, "When Bearing Witness Overrides a Reporter's Fear," *Nieman Reports*, June 22, 2006.

"went into black . . .": *Ghosts by Daylight*, 173.

"hand-to-mouth . . .": Janine di Giovanni, interview with author.

"never wanted to be . . .": Janine di Giovanni, interview with author.

Robin Wright

"The Islamists are . . .": Robin Wright, ed., *The Islamists Are Coming: Who They Really Are* (Washington, DC: United States Institute of Peace, 2012).

Robin Wright wanted to be like: Robin Wright, interview with author, August 21, 2012.

"Maybe I'll go off . . .": Ibid.

"I was the only one . . .": Ibid.

"broke the story . . .": Ibid.

"The things you are . . .": Ibid.

"mercenary groupies": Murray, "Marguerite Higgins," 231.

"This reporter was . . .": Robin Wright, "Reporter Describes Rout of FNLA from Angola Town," *Christian Science Monitor*, February 9, 1976.

"a memorable week": Robin Wright, interview with author, August 21, 2012.

"If you know enough . . .": Ibid.

"All the change in . . .": Ibid.

"All these events . . .": Ibid.

"For many young . . .": Robin Wright, "The Pink Hijab," *Wilson Quarterly* 35, no. 3 (Summer 2011), 47–51.

"A lot of big-name . . .": Robin Wright, interview with author, August 21, 2012.

She never married: Ibid.

Third World kids: Ibid.

"Know the world . . .": Ibid.

"I tell young people . . .": Ibid.

Martha Raddatz

"The one reason . . .": Martha Raddatz, "From War Zones to the White House," speech at Kenyon College, Gambier, OH, October 20, 2012, Video, 1:00, www.youtube.com/watch?v=OUbK_1cFf8Q.

"Bin Laden was ordered . . .": "Mission at Hand—GMA," www.mydaily.com/2011/05/02/mission-at-hand.

"absolutely no inkling": Martha Raddatz, interview with author, November 1, 2012.

"I liked to read . . .": Ibid.

"Before she was Martha . . .": Kevin Cullen, "Accentuate Candidates, Eliminate Moderator," *Boston Globe*, October 13, 2012.

"I remember thinking . . .": Martha Raddatz, interview with author.

"US Navy warships . . .": Barbara Starr and Martha Raddatz, "Navy Reacts to Possible Terror Threat," ABC News, June 21, 2001, http://abcnews.go.com/International/story?id=80879&page=1.

"The State Department . . .": Martha Raddatz, "Watching the Pentagon Burn: ABC's Martha Raddatz Remembers 9/11," ABC News, September 9, 2011, http://abcnews.go.com/blogs

/headlines/2011/09/watching-the-pentagon-burn-abcs
-martha-raddatz-remembers-911/.

"I spent the day . . .": Ibid.

"platoon pindown": "Martha Raddatz: ABC News White House
Correspondent: Letter Written by Martha Raddatz's Daugh-
ter," *Q&A,* C-Span, September 17, 2006, www.q-and-a.org
/Transcript/?ProgramID=1093.

"I knew 8 soldiers . . .": Ibid.

"I think you take . . .": Raddatz, interview with author.

"No one asks . . .": Martha Raddatz, "Martha Raddatz Por-
trays a Platoon Under Fire," NPR, January 15, 2008, www.
npr.org/2008/01/15/17979692/martha-raddatz-portrays
-a-platoon-under-fire.

"searingly vivid evidence . . .": Janet Maslin, "Visceral Tales from
Iraq, Where Life-Changing Days Are Just the Start of Pain,"
New York Times, March 12, 2007, www.nytimes.com/2007/03
/12/books/12masl.html?pagewanted=all&_r=0.

"I say things they . . .": Raddatz, "From War Zones to the White
House."

She is not sure she: "Letter Written by Martha Raddatz's Daughter," Q&A.

"My mom began to cry . . .": Greta Bradlee, "Point of View," University of California–Berkeley News, www.berkeley.edu
/news/media/releases/2006/02/06_bradlee.shtml.

"My mother's own . . .": Ibid.

"We've got a country . . .": Raddatz, "From War Zones to the
White House."

"One of the stresses . . .": Raddatz, interview with author.

"Multiple deployments . . .": "The Backstory: The Untold Military
Stories," interview with Martha Raddatz, *Washington Week,*
PBS online, video, 4:46, www.pbs.org/weta/washington
week/content/backstory-untold-military-stories.

Bibliography

General Overview

Atwood, Kathryn J. *Women Heroes of World War II: 26 Stories of Espionage, Sabotage, Resistance, and Rescue*. Chicago: Chicago Review Press, 2011.

Bartimus, Tad, Denby Fawcett, Jurate Kazickas, Edith Lederer, Ann Bryan Mariano, Anne Morrissy Merick, Laura Palmer, Kate Webb, Tracy Wood. *War Torn: Stories of War from the Women Reporters Who Covered Vietnam*. New York: Random House, 2002.

Brannen, Beverly. "Helen Johns Kirtland" Biographical Essay. Library of Congress. www.loc.gov./rr/print/coll/womphotoj /Kirtlandessay.pdf

Colman, Penny. *Where the Action Was: Women War Correspondents in World War II*. New York: Crown Publishers, 2002.

Edwards, Julia. *Women of the World: The Great Foreign Correspondents*. Boston: Houghton Mifflin, 1988.

Gourley, Catherine. *War, Women, and the News : How Female Journalists Won the Battle to Cover World War II*. New York: Atheneum Books for Young Readers, 2007.

Hoffman, Joyce. *On Their Own: Women Journalists and the American Experience in Vietnam*. Cambridge, MA: Da Capo Press, 2008.

Price-Groff, Claire. *Extraordinary Women Journalists*. New York: Children's Press, 1997.

Sorel, Nancy Caldwell. *The Women Who Wrote the War*. New York: Arcade Publishing, 1999.

War Correspondents (as introduced in text)

Peggy Hull

Benjamin, Robert Spiers, ed., *Eye Witness*. New York: Alliance Book Corporation, 1940.

Smith, Wilda M. and Eleanor A. Bogart. *The Wars of Peggy Hull: The Life and Times of a War Correspondent*. El Paso: Texas Western Press, 1991.

Louise Bryant

Bryant, Louise. *Six Red Months in Russia: An Observer's Account of Russia Before and During the Proletarian Dictatorship*. New York: George H. Doran, 1918.

Bessie Beatty

Beatty, Bessie. *The Red Heart of Russia*. New York: Century Co., 1918.

Rheta Childe Dorr

Dorr, Rheta Childe. *A Woman of Fifty*. New York: Funk & Wagnalls Co., 1924

Dorr, Rheta Childe. *Inside the Russian Revolution*. New York: Arno Press, 1970.

Irene Corbally Kuhn

Kuhn, Irene Corbally. *Assigned to Adventure.* Philadelphia: J. B. Lippencott, 1938.

Kuhn, Irene Corbally. "Shanghai: The Way it Was: A Glance Back at a Short, But Extraordinary Era," *Los Angeles Times,* October 19, 1986. *http://articles.latimes.com/1986-10-19 /magazine/tm-5888_1_vintage-shanghai.*

Kuhn, Irene. "Tea and Ashes." In *Deadline Delayed* by Overseas Press Club of America, 268–281. New York: E. P. Dutton & Co., 1947.

Sigrid Schultz

Schultz, Sigrid Lillian. "Angora: Pictorial Records of an SS Experiment." *Wisconsin Magazine of History* 50, no. 4 (Summer 1967): 392–413.

Schultz, Sigrid Lillian. *Germany Will Try It Again.* New York: Reynal and Hitchcock, 1944.

Shirer, William. *Berlin Diary: The Journal of a Foreign Correspondent, 1934–1941.* New York: A. A. Knopf, 1941.

Dorothy Thompson

Kurth, Peter. *American Cassandra: The Life of Dorothy Thompson.* Boston: Little, Brown, 1990.

Sanders, Marion K. *Dorothy Thompson: A Legend in Her Time.* Boston: Houghton Mifflin, 1973.

Thompson, Dorothy. "Goodbye to Germany." *Harper's,* December 1932, 43–51.

Thompson, Dorothy. "I Saw Hitler." *Cosmopolitan,* March 1932, 32–33, 160–163.

Martha Gellhorn

Gellhorn, Martha. "Dachau Experimental Murder." *Colliers Weekly,* June 23, 1945, 16.

Gellhorn, Martha. "Only the Shells Whine." *Collier's Weekly,* July 17, 1937, 12–13, 64–65.

Gellhorn, Martha. *Travels with Myself and Another.* New York: Jeremy P. Tarcher/Putnam, 2001.

Gellhorn, Martha. *The View from the Ground.* New York: Atlantic Monthly Press, 1988.

Lynn, Kenneth Schuyler. *Hemingway.* New York: Simon and Schuster, 1987.

Moorehead, Caroline, ed., *Selected Letters of Martha Gellhorn.* New York: H. Holt, 2006

Margaret Bourke-White

Bourke-White, Margaret. *"Dear Fatherland, Rest Quietly": A Report on the Collapse of Hitler's "Thousand Years."* New York: Simon and Schuster, 1946.

Bourke-White, Margaret. *Portrait of Myself.* New York: Simon and Schuster, 1963.

Callahan, Sean. *Margaret Bourke-White: Photographer.* Boston: Little, Brown, 1998.

Marguerite Higgins

Beech, Keyes. *Tokyo and Points East.* New York: Doubleday, 1954.

Higgins, Marguerite. *News is a Singular Thing.* New York: Doubleday, 1955.

Higgins, Marguerite and Carl Mydans. *War in Korea: The Report of a Woman Combat Correspondent.* New York: Doubleday, 1951.

Gloria Emerson

Emerson, Gloria. "Buddhist Monks Quietly Lead Campaign Against Thieu." *New York Times,* September 3, 1971.

Emerson, Gloria. "Even the Postcards in Saigon Depict G.I.'s in Battle." *New York Times,* March 7, 1970.

Emerson, Gloria. "On Med-Evac Copter, Faces and Pain; Calm but Weary." *New York Times,* June 2, 1970.

Emerson, Gloria. "Vietnamese General and a G.I. Who Want to See Victory." *New York Times,* February 17, 1971.

Emerson, Gloria. *Winners & Losers: Battles, Retreats, Gains, Losses and Ruins from the Vietnam War.* New York: Random House, 1976.

Georgie Anne Geyer

Geyer, Georgie Anne. *Buying the Night Flight: The Autobiography of a Woman Foreign Correspondent.* New York: Delacorte Press/Seymour Lawrence, 1983.

Syndicated newspaper column archive. "Georgie Anne Geyer." www.uexpress.com/georgieannegeyer/.

Janine di Giovanni

di Giovanni, Janine. *Ghosts by Daylight: Love, War, and Redemption.* New York: Alfred A Knopf, 2011.

di Giovanni, Janine. *Madness Visible: A Memoir of War.* New York: Alfred A. Knopf, 2003.

Janine di Giovanni website. "Janine di Giovanni, Journalist and Author." http://*www.janinedigiovanni.com.*

Robin Wright

Wright, Robin B. *Rock the Casbah: Rage and Rebellion Across the Islamic World.* New York: Simon and Schuster, 2011.

Robin Wright website. "Robin Wright Books." www.robinwright.net/.

Martha Raddatz

Raddatz, Martha. "From War Zones to the White House." Filmed at Kenyon College on October 20, 2012. YouTube video, 1:00:35. Posted February 26, 2013. www.youtube.com/watch?v=OUbK_1cFf8Q/.

Raddatz, Martha. *The Long Road Home: A Story of War and Family.* New York: G. P. Putnam's Sons, 2007.

Index